Va va Voom
Vegan Cakes

Va va Voom Vegan Cakes

More than 50 recipes for vegan-friendly bakes
that not only taste great but look amazing!

ANGELA ROMEO

photography by
CLARE WINFIELD

RYLAND PETERS & SMALL
LONDON • NEW YORK

For Giuseppe, Elena & Sofia

Senior Designer Toni Kay
Editor Kate Reeves-Brown
Production Manager
 Gordana Simakovic
Art Director Leslie Harrington
Editorial Director Julia Charles
Publisher Cindy Richards

Food stylist Angela Romeo
Prop stylist Max Robinson
Indexer Hilary Bird

First published in 2021 by Ryland
Peters & Small
20–21 Jockey's Fields, London
WC1R 4BW
and
341 E 116th St, New York
NY 10029
www.rylandpeters.com

10 9 8 7 6 5 4 3 2 1

Text copyright © Angela Romeo
Design and photographs copyright
© Ryland Peters & Small 2021

ISBN: 978-1-78879-378-0

Printed in China

The author's moral rights have
been asserted. All rights reserved.
No part of this publication may be
reproduced, stored in a retrieval
system or transmitted in any
form or by any means, electronic,
mechanical, photocopying or
otherwise, without the prior
permission of the publisher.

A CIP record for this book is available
from the British Library.

US Library of Congress Cataloging-in-
Publication Data has been applied for.

Notes:
• Both British (Metric) and American
(Imperial plus US cups) measurements
are included in these recipes for your
convenience, however it is important
to work with one set of measurements
and not alternate between the two
within a recipe.
• All spoon measurements are level
unless otherwise specified. A teaspoon
of liquid is 5 ml, a tablespoon is 15 ml.
• Ovens should be preheated to the
specified temperatures. We recommend
using an oven thermometer. If using a
fan-assisted oven, adjust temperatures
according to the manufacturer's
instructions.
• When a recipe calls for the grated
zest of citrus fruit, buy unwaxed fruit
and wash well before using.

Contents

Introduction

The only thing better than a show-stopping, crowd-pleasing cake... is a show-stopping, crowd-pleasing, vegan cake! To hear gasps of joy for the look and taste of vegan cake is fabulous! It's also brilliant on a practical level (not just on building my ego!), if making for a special occasion, it will optimize the number of people who can enjoy it – limiting the need to bake separate cakes. No one need be left out!

Surely I'm going to need lots of specialist shops for striking and delicious vegan cakes? I set myself the challenge that this didn't need to be the case. Vegan or not, the base recipes in this book are great 'go-to' recipes – the perfect foundation for the ultimate wow-factor celebration cake, cute cupcakes or a fabulous 'just because' cake. Take inspiration from the designs in this book and complete with that all-important touch of va va voom!

The classic flavoured cakes in this book are working that cake-plate in the style-stakes! But it's also been great to develop recipes with refreshing new flavour combinations complemented by vegan decorations that reflect those flavours. Think flaked coconut creating an elegant white border, vibrant carrot curl cake toppers and colour pops of red from deliberately placed raspberries, giving both a fresh artistic and delicious look.

The most important thing is to have fun with the flavours and designs in this book. Happy plant-based baking... and of course eating!

Angela
x

TIPS, TECHNIQUES & FINISHING TOUCHES

VEGAN BAKING SUPERSTARS

Having a few of these to hand, along with store cupboard staples, such as flour and sugar, means you'll be able to whip up a vegan treat any time!

SOYA/SOY YOGURT

Soya/soy yogurt gives an unbelievable soft texture to vegan cakes. Mixed with vegetable or sunflower oil, it not only gives fantastic results, but by simply mixing with the other wet ingredients of a cake batter, then adding to the dry ingredients, it also makes for a super-speedy method. A wonderful base for great-tasting show-stopper cakes.

SOYA/SOY MILK

Mixing soya/soy milk with lemon juice makes a homemade vegan buttermilk. Reacting with bicarbonate of soda/baking soda and baking powder, it's great for creating light and airy cakes that still retain their shape and structure.

CHICKPEAS/GARBANZO BEANS

Chickpea/garbanzo bean water, also known as aquafaba, is a fantastic replacement for egg white. It reacts in a similar way due to its high protein content. Super handy to have to hand for every vegan baker, perfect for light meringues. A stabilizer like distilled white vinegar will help keep whipped meringue peaks glossy and firm.

SUNFLOWER OIL

This oil is so versatile. It doesn't have a strong flavour, comes from one flower/seed source and is light in colour – it's an all-round winner for oil-based cake batter.

PLANT/VEGAN BUTTER

More readily available than ever, a great straight replacement for butter. It works wonders for buttercream. I would even, dare I say, put it out there and say that it actually pipes with better results! After a few hours it even 'crusts' over, so holds well like a traditional buttercream-covered cake would. Adding a tablespoon or two of water to loosen vegan buttercream works really well too and means the cake can keep well, covered at room temperature – there's no need to chill it. Vegan margarine, however, does need to be chilled, so do not use this for buttercream or you may end up with a slippery-slidey mess on your hands!

GOLDEN/LIGHT CORN SYRUP

It's always going to have a place for drizzling on porridge and making flapjacks, but this little gem has had a bit of a makeover and taken the vegan cake baking world by storm, too. It has a little more depth of flavour than caster sugar, complementing naturally sweet vegan-friendly products such as soya/soy milk and soya/soy yogurt.

CASHEW NUTS

Soaked and blended, these little beauties make the most amazing light and fluffy 'buttercream'. Lighter than classic buttercream, if used between layers, it's good to mix with chopped nuts or fruit to maintain height and strength, or combine with vegan buttercream when holding up several layers of cake for a delicious and sturdy show-stopper.

COCONUT OIL

When warmed, coconut oil is fantastic for thinning sweet sauces that you need to solidify a little when at room temperature – great for perfecting your drizzle on drip cakes! If you're in a sticky situation when melting chocolate and it becomes thick, stir through a touch of coconut oil – it should melt and loosen up the chocolate once again.

COCOA POWDER

Wow. Just wow. It gives the most chocolatey cake you can wish for without the need for vegan chocolate. I never really appreciated the power of humble cocoa powder before writing this book!

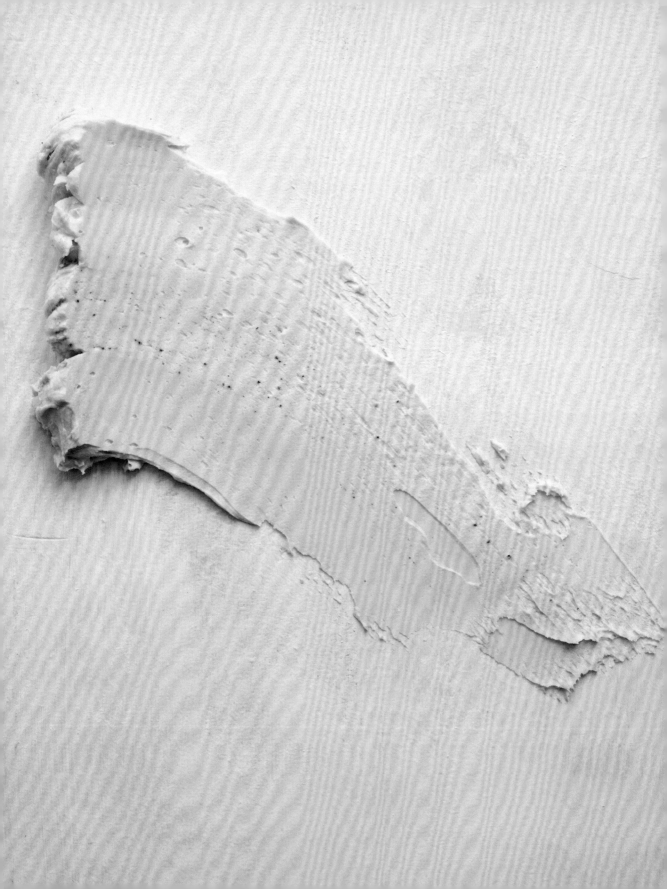

TIPS:

PAN-TASTIC LINE UP

Greasing and lining a cake pan can be tricky if you do not have vegan butter or margarine to hand, especially if the batter you're using uses vegetable/sunflower oil. Grease and line the base using the sunflower oil and baking parchment, then cut the baking parchment strips for the sides to size. When the cake mix is ready, dot the inside edges of the pan with four dots of the mix and use to secure the strips in place.

GO HALVES

If you love a design in this book, but want a smaller cake, you can always scale the recipe down. If it's a large two-layer cake using 2 x 20-cm/8-inch pans, simply halve the batter ingredients and cook in 1 x 20-cm/8-inch pan for the time specified in the recipe to make a single layer version (omit or adjust the filling and coating accordingly).

STIR IT UP!

As scary as it may seem… sometimes you have to chuck out the baking rule book! It's quite a different technique mixing batter for vegan bakes. When mixing wet and dry ingredients together, once the flour-part has disappeared, it's time to stop stirring. There's no need for an electric whisk; it is too harsh for most vegan batters and can create a dense, even sunken, cake. A folding technique with a rubber spatula is a great way to combine the wet and dry ingredients. Continue this folding technique when adding any fruit, nuts or any extras at the end, and all will be fine!

ALL GOOD THINGS…

You may notice that once your vegan cakes are cooled, particularly small cakes like cupcakes, they may have a very thin crust. After cooling, transfer to a plastic airtight container (or for larger cakes wrap in clingfilm/plastic wrap) for a couple of hours… And voila! Soft tops! Obviously, if you are trimming the tops, or completely covering with icing/frosting, use as soon as they are cool.

COLOUR ME BEAUTIFUL

Get experimenting with natural colours! Try pouches of coloured wonder, such as pitaya and spirulina superfood powders, or go for store-cupboard brights, such as turmeric and beetroot/beet. There are also lots of good vegan pastes and gels readily available.

Pink – Dragon fruit powder/pitaya powder.
Orange – To colour around 450 g/1 lb. of icing/frosting a mid-orange, stir 2 teaspoons 'crushed' raw beetroot/beet (use the rough small star-shaped holes on a box grater for this) into vegan buttercream along with 2 teaspoons turmeric (see note), 2½ teaspoons cinnamon and ½ teaspoon pure vanilla extract (adding the cinnamon and extra vanilla overpowers any taste from the turmeric and also tastes great alongside a spiced cake).
Peach – A little pitaya powder and a dash of ground turmeric (see note).
Yellow – A touch of turmeric (see note) works wonders in enhancing the yellow hue of buttercream. For lemon yellow royal icing, replace water with passion fruit pulp (sieve to remove the seeds, if liked).
Green – A touch of matcha powder.
Blue – A sprinkling of spirulina powder.
Lilac – Playing around with purple! Mix ⅛ teaspoon pink pitaya powder and ⅛ teaspoon blue spirulina powder into 325 g/11 oz. of buttercream to achieve a lilac shade.
Note: Be careful of using light-coloured cake plates here, as turmeric can stain. A disposable cake board is also a good option.

NATURAL BLING!

All things bright and beautiful… well edible ones! Don't forget to look directly to nature for colour inspiration, from edible and/or food-safe flowers and deep red and purple berries to fresh green herbs, and not forgetting zingy zesty colours from oranges, lemons and limes. All can make beautiful focal points on both large and small cakes.

BUTTERCREAM –
SMOOTH OPERATOR

CRUMB COATING

1 A spoonful of icing/frosting spread onto the middle of the cake board will stop the cake moving around while you're working.

2 When crumb coating it's best to apply the buttercream little and often; this will help to give an even distribution and prevent dragging the crumbs around the cake. Use the tip of a dinner knife to apply buttercream to the sides and top of your stacked cake, slightly spreading a little more buttercream into any gaps or recesses, if necessary.

3 Smooth the top with a palette knife/metal spatula. At this stage, the sides do not need to be completely smooth.

4 When the cake is covered, take the palette knife/metal spatula or a cake scraper and sweep around the cake with a little pressure to remove the excess buttercream. Scrape the buttercream into a separate bowl (as it may have crumbs in) and continue to remove the excess buttercream. If there are any gaps or holes, fill with a little buttercream and smooth again.

5 After finishing the sides you will have little peaks at the top edge of the cake. Use an off-set palette knife/metal spatula, held horizontally, to draw these peaks to the centre of the cake, using gentle but sturdy sweeping motions. Chill the crumb-coated cake for 15 minutes.

FINAL COAT

After the cake has chilled, use the same technique as crumb coating for the final coat. However, when using your palette knife/metal spatula or cake scraper, apply slightly less pressure, aiming to 'spread' the buttercream around the cake whilst maintaining straight sides.

WELL EQUIPPED

CAKE PANS

Lots of the cakes in this book use 18-cm/7-inch round cake pans (make sure they are at least 4.5 cm/2 inches in height). If you have only two 18-cm/7-inch cake pans, the sponge mixture will hold while the other sponges are baking, so you can bake in batches. Cover the remaining batter in clingfilm/plastic wrap, until ready to bake.

RUBBER SPATULA

Not only great for ensuring every last bit of batter is scraped from the bowl, but perfect for folding together batter ingredients.

PALETTE KNIVES/ METAL SPATULAS

A long palette knife/metal spatula is perfect for smoothing buttercream. A medium-sized palette knife/metal spatula is fantastic to use for making patterns on a buttercream-covered cake if you are working your confidence up to super smooth sides. Lightly press vertically, swiping up and down for a striking ridge effect for example.

WEIGHING SCALES

It may seem obvious, but weighing scales with a tare 0 function makes making the basic Vegan Chocolate Sponge (see page 16) and Vegan Deep Vanilla Sponge (see page 15) super easy. Weigh out all the dry ingredients in one bowl, then weigh out all the liquid ingredients in another, before adding the wet to the dry.

FOOD PROCESSOR

I have given the technique for making buttercream with a hand-held electric whisk. If you do have a food processor, however, this is a super-easy way for whizzing it up instantly and minimizing clouds of icing/confectioners' sugar. Put all the ingredients in the food processor and pulse until smooth.

COCKTAIL STICKS/TOOTHPICKS

Perfect for checking sponge in shallower cakes is cooked without creating a big hole.

BASIC RECIPES

Vegan deep vanilla sponge

A delightfully soft, versatile sponge. Use for everything from stylish cupcakes to large show-stoppers - also the perfect base to allow additional flavours to sing!

480 g/3²/₃ cups plain/
  all-purpose flour
280 g/scant 1¹/₂ cups caster/
  superfine sugar
4 teaspoons baking powder
2 teaspoons bicarbonate
  of soda/baking soda
480 g/2¹/₄ cups soya/
  soy yogurt
180 ml/³/₄ cup sunflower oil
2 tablespoons golden/
  light corn syrup
2 teaspoons pure vanilla
  extract

Makes enough for 1 large cake

Preheat the oven to 180°C (350°F) Gas 4.

Sift the flour into a large bowl, add the sugar, baking powder and bicarbonate of soda/baking soda, and mix with a spoon to combine. Make a well in the middle.

Put the yogurt into a bowl with the sunflower oil, golden/light corn syrup and vanilla extract. Mix with a spoon until fully combined. Pour into the well of dry ingredients. Fold through with a spatula or wooden spoon until just combined and smooth.

Vegan chocolate sponge

Maximum impact with minimal fuss. Using only a handful of ingredients, this chocolatey sponge gives luxurious flavour and unbeatable texture.

480 g/3^2/$_3$ cups plain/
  all-purpose flour
5^1/$_2$ tablespoons unsweetened
  cocoa powder
280 g/scant 1^1/$_2$ cups caster/
  superfine sugar
5 teaspoons baking powder
1^1/$_2$ teaspoons bicarbonate
  of soda/baking soda
480 g/2^1/$_4$ cups soya/
  soy yogurt
180 ml/^{3}/$_4$ cup sunflower oil
2 tablespoons golden/
  light corn syrup

Makes enough
for 1 large cake

Preheat the oven to 180°C (350°F) Gas 4.

Sift the flour into a large bowl, add the cocoa powder, sugar, baking powder and bicarbonate of soda/baking soda, and mix with a spoon to combine. Make a well in the middle.

Put the yogurt into a bowl with the sunflower oil and golden/light corn syrup. Mix with a spoon until fully combined. Pour into the well of dry ingredients. Fold through with a spatula or wooden spoon until just combined and smooth.

Vegan terrific traybake sponge

This simple traybake sponge mixture is perfect for baking little squares of joy!

320 ml/1⅓ cups soya/soy milk

3 tablespoons freshly squeezed lemon juice

350 g/2⅔ cups plain/all-purpose flour

½ teaspoon bicarbonate of soda/baking soda

4 teaspoons baking powder

200 g/1 cup caster/superfine sugar

175 g/6 oz. vegan butter, melted

1 teaspoon pure vanilla extract

Makes enough for a 30 x 20-cm/12 x 8-inch pan

Preheat the oven to 180°C (350°F) Gas 4.

Put the soya/soy milk and lemon juice into a jug/cup or bowl, mix well and set aside until thickened.

Meanwhile, sift the flour into a large bowl, add the bicarbonate of soda/baking soda, baking powder and sugar; mix together. Add the melted vegan butter, the vanilla extract and half the milk and lemon juice mix.

Fold with a rubber spatula until it's just combined and smooth, then add the remaining soya/soy milk and lemon juice, mixing in 2–3 tablespoons at a time, continuing to use a folding technique between each addition.

Top tip

Grease and line the pan with baking parchment. With the long side facing you, allow the top and bottom of the parchment to overhang the two long sides. If your pan is non-stick, this should be enough. If not, stick a small strip of parchment to each of the shorter sides.

Simple vegan vanilla buttercream

A great covering for celebration and party cakes. Add a swirl to cupcakes and have every occasion covered. No-one need be left out of the party!

500 g/1 lb. 2 oz. vegan butter, cubed and softened
2 teaspoons pure vanilla extract
1 kg/8 cups icing/confectioners' sugar

Makes 1.5 kg/3¼ lb.

Place the vegan butter in a bowl with the vanilla extract, 2 tablespoons of water and a few large spoonfuls of the icing/confectioners' sugar.

Whisk with a hand-held electric whisk until combined, then whisk in the remaining icing/confectioners' sugar in manageable batches until smooth and spreadable. Add another 1 tablespoon of water, if necessary.

Top tip
If scaling down this recipe, reduce the vanilla extract to taste and adjust the water accordingly. Very small quantities may not need any water.

Vegan cream cheese frosting

Get that unbeatable cheesecake flavour in an instant. Who doesn't want to smother that on their cake?!

500 g/1 lb. 2 oz. vegan cream cheese
70 g/½ cup icing/confectioners' sugar

Makes enough to fill and top 1 large cake

Put the vegan cream cheese in a bowl. Sift over the icing/confectioners' sugar and whisk with a hand-held electric whisk until combined.

Chill in the fridge for at least 30 minutes until firmed up a little, then fill and/or ice your cake and chill the filled/iced cake(s) for at least 30 minutes or until ready to serve.

Vegan chocolate fudge frosting

As if by magic, soya/soy yogurt, cocoa powder, vegan butter and icing sugar come together to make this indulgent, smooth, rich fudge frosting.

125 g/4 oz. vegan butter, softened and cubed
150 g/1½ cups unsweetened cocoa powder, sifted
2 teaspoons pure vanilla extract
330 g/1½ cups soya/ soy yogurt
190 g/1⅓ cups icing/ confectioners' sugar, sifted

Makes enough to coat 1 large cake

Put the butter in a bowl with the cocoa, vanilla extract, half the yogurt and half the icing/ confectioners' sugar. Whisk with a hand-held electric whisk until thick and smooth. Add the remaining icing/confectioners' sugar and remaining yogurt and whisk until smooth and glossy.

Cashew nut vanilla frosting

A vegan baking classic, why not get experimenting; blend until super smooth or blend for a little less time for a touch of texture.

600 g/5 cups raw cashews
100 ml/scant ½ cup soya/ soy milk or almond milk
3 tablespoons golden/ light corn syrup
2 teaspoons pure vanilla extract

Makes 1 kg/2¼ lb.

Soak the cashews in water overnight. Drain and rinse the cashews and pat dry. Blend in a food processor with the remaining ingredients until smooth; this will take at least 10 minutes.

You may need to do this in batches. If so, transfer the first batch to a large bowl, then repeat with the remaining ingredients. Combine the two batches with a hand-held electric whisk (add more soya/ soy milk or almond milk if necessary). If the mixture has become quite warm in the food processor, chill for 30–60 minutes until firm enough to hold its shape if piped.

Vegan Royal icing

Drip and drizzle decoratively onto your cakes to your heart's content with this super-bright, super-luxurious icing.

5 tablespoons chickpea/
    garbanzo bean water,
    plus extra if needed
300 g/generous 2 cups icing/
    confectioners' sugar, sifted,
    plus extra if needed

Makes enough to top and decorate 1 large cake

Whisk the chickpea/garbanzo bean water with a hand-held electric whisk until foamy, then add 200 g/1½ cups of the icing/confectioners' sugar to the mixture and continue to mix on high until the mixture is thick and glossy.

Add the rest of the sugar and 1 teaspoon of water, and whisk again until thick and glossy. Whisk in another 1 teaspoon of water to loosen (or a little more icing/confectioners' sugar to thicken), if necessary.

Soft vegan caramel sauce

With a slight saltiness from the almond butter, this caramel sauce is truly addictive! Why not make a double-batch and serve some on the side!

60 g/2¼ oz. almond butter
2 tablespoons golden/
    light corn syrup
20 g/¾ oz. coconut oil

Makes enough to top one large cake

In a bowl, mix the almond butter and golden/light corn syrup together.

Heat the coconut oil in a small bowl in the microwave for 20–40 seconds, stirring every 20 seconds, until melted, or heat in a bain marie until melted.

Gradually stir the melted coconut oil into the almond butter mix.

Vegan meringue

So satisfying! Knowing these sweet little meringue kisses, roses and stars contain no egg white, they give me a kick of delight every time I make them!

120 ml/½ cup chickpea/
garbanzo bean water
½ teaspoon white distilled
vinegar
125 g/⅔ cup caster/
superfine sugar

Makes approx
25 meringue kisses

Preheat the oven to 110°C (225°F) Gas ¼.

Whisk the chickpea/garbanzo bean water and distilled vinegar to soft peaks.

Add the sugar and whisk for 5–7 minutes until stiff. Use as specified in each recipe.

Vegan biscuit/cookie thins

A perfectly crisp biscuit, this little baking super-star holds well whilst baking – great for cutting into any shape you like.

50 g/2 oz. vegan butter, cubed
50 g/¼ cup caster/superfine
sugar
2 tablespoons soya/soy yogurt
135 g/1 cup self-raising/
self-rising flour
½–1 teaspoon soya/soy milk,
if needed

Makes 12 medium
biscuits/cookies

Cream the vegan butter and sugar together with a hand-held electric whisk. Gradually whisk in the yogurt. Sift over the flour and stir until it clumps together, adding the soya/soy milk if needed.

Press into a ball of dough. Wrap in clingfilm/plastic wrap and chill for 15 minutes. Use as specified in each recipe (see tip).

Top tip
This dough is best shaped straight away as specified in each recipe. However, you can get ahead by cutting the shapes and then popping them, covered, into the fridge for up to 24 hours. Cooked biscuits/cookies will last up to 3 days in an airtight container.

Tutti Frutti

Lemon meringue mini cakes

The vegan lemon curd in these zingy cupcakes is so easy to make and tastes amazing. Make a double batch; it is delicious on warm toast!

1 quantity of Vegan Meringue (see page 27), made just before piping – this mix is best used immediately
grated zest of 1 lemon
½ quantity of Vegan Deep Vanilla Sponge mixture (see page 15)

LEMON CURD
115 ml/½ cup soya/soy milk
1 tablespoon cornflour/cornstarch
100 g/½ cup caster/superfine sugar

60 ml/4 tablespoons freshly squeezed lemon juice
grated zest of 1 lemon
⅛ teaspoon turmeric powder
2 baking sheets, lined
5-cm/2-inch round cutter
piping/pastry bag fitted with a large star nozzle/tip
12-hole muffin pan, lined with cases
mini cake sparklers (optional)

Makes 10–12

For the meringue toppers preheat the oven to 120°C (240°F) Gas ½. Take the lined baking sheets and, with a pencil, draw 9 circles on each sheet of parchment, using the cutter as a guide. Turn them over, pencil-side down.

Fill the piping/pastry bag with the meringue mix and pipe swirled 'mounds' of the mixture on the lined baking sheets, using the circles as guides. Bake for 1 hour 40 minutes until the undersides are dry and lift easily from the parchment (you will not need all of these, but it's good to have a few spare).

For the lemon curd, mix 1 tablespoon of the soya/soy milk with the cornflour/cornstarch to make a paste. Put the sugar in a small pan with the remaining milk, the lemon juice and the lemon zest. Heat gently until the sugar has dissolved. Add the cornflour/cornstarch paste and turmeric, and continue to cook, whisking continuously and increasing the heat slightly until it thickens; about 5 minutes. Pour into a sterilized jar until ready to use. (If not using right away, cool, seal or cover and store in the fridge.)

For the cakes, preheat the oven to 180°C (350°F) Gas 4.

Stir the lemon zest through the sponge mixture. Divide between the paper cases until two-thirds full. Bake in the preheated oven for 25 minutes until an inserted cocktail stick/toothpick comes out clean. Allow to cool in the muffin pan for 10 minutes, then place on a wire rack to cool completely.

Level the very tops of the cupcakes with a knife, if necessary. Use a teaspoon to remove a little piece of cake from the middle of each. Fill with the lemon curd, then spread a little extra curd on top of each cupcake. Top with a meringue. Serve each with a mini cake sparkler, if liked.

Banana Bundt cake with butterscotch

My family are bananas about bananas, so I simply had to take the banana bread craze to the next level with a huge banana Bundt cake – topped with vegan butterscotch and banana chips for good measure!

300 g/10½ oz. (approx. 3) very ripe bananas, mashed
1 quantity of Vegan Deep Vanilla Sponge mixture (see page 15)
35 g/½ cup banana chips/ dried banana slices
icing/confectioners' sugar, for dusting (optional)

BUTTERSCOTCH
60 g/2¼ oz. vegan butter
90 g/scant ½ cup Demerara/ raw sugar
½ teaspoon flaked sea salt
50 ml/3½ tablespoons soya/soy milk
1 teaspoon pure vanilla extract
23-cm/9-inch (1.5–1.75-litre/ 50–60-fl. oz.) Bundt pan, greased

Serves 20

Fold the mashed bananas through the sponge mixture until combined.

Spoon into the greased Bundt pan (leave at least 4 cm/ 1¾ inches of space at the top of the pan – you may not need all the mix), bake for 1 hour–1 hour 10 minutes until an inserted cocktail stick/toothpick comes out clean. Allow to cool in the pan for 10 minutes, then remove and place on a wire rack to cool completely. Trim the flat top of the cake so it is level, then invert onto a serving plate so that the flat top becomes the base.

For the butterscotch, melt the vegan butter in a pan over a medium heat. Add the Demerara/raw sugar, salt and soya/soy milk. Bring the mixture to the boil, scraping down the sides occasionally and simmer for 4–5 minutes.

Remove from the heat and stir through the vanilla extract. The butterscotch will thicken on cooling; avoid simmering for too long or it may end up too thick to pour.

Allow to mostly cool, then drizzle over the cake. Decorate with the banana chips/dried banana slices. Dust with icing/confectioners' sugar, if using.

Coconut & passion fruit cake

I love eating tropical fruits in the colder months, just the hit of fragrant passion fruit takes me straight to warmer climates. The added bonus here is that the pulp naturally gives the glacé icing on this cake a gorgeous lemony colour!

400 g/3 cups plain/
all-purpose flour
280 g/scant 1½ cups
caster/superfine sugar
80 g/generous 1 cup
desiccated/dried
unsweetened shredded
coconut
5 teaspoons baking powder
2 teaspoons bicarbonate
of soda/baking soda
480 g/2¼ cups soya/soy yogurt
180 ml/¾ cup sunflower oil
2 tablespoons golden/
light corn syrup
2 passion fruit, pulp
and seeds

COATING
825 g/1 lb. 13 oz. Simple
Vegan Vanilla Buttercream
(see page 20), made with
275 g/9½ oz. vegan butter
and 550 g/scant 4 cups
icing/confectioners' sugar
vegan purple food colouring
(optional, see colour tip)

DECORATION
40 g/1 cup flaked coconut
100 g/¾ cup icing/
confectioners' sugar, sifted
25 g/1 oz. passion fruit
pulp and seeds (approx.
1 passion fruit), plus
3 passion fruit, halved
3 pineapple leaves (optional)
2 x deep 20-cm/8-inch cake
pans, greased and lined
1 wooden skewer

Serves 20

Preheat the oven to 180°C (350°F) Gas 4.

Sift the flour into a large bowl, add the caster/superfine sugar, coconut, baking powder and bicarbonate of soda/baking soda, and mix with a spoon to combine. Make a well in the middle.

Put the soya/soy yogurt into a bowl, add the sunflower oil and golden/light corn syrup. Mix with a spoon until fully combined. Pour into the well of dry ingredients. Fold through with a spatula or wooden spoon until combined and smooth. Fold through the passion fruit pulp and seeds until fully combined.

Transfer to the greased and lined pans. Bake in the preheated oven for 45–50 minutes until an inserted cocktail stick/toothpick comes out clean. Leave to cool in the pans for 10 minutes, then transfer to wire racks to cool completely.

Trim the tops of the cakes to make level, if necessary. Sandwich the cakes together using 200 g/7 oz. of the buttercream – the bottom side of the top cake should be facing up. Place the cake on a cake board. Crumb coat (see page 12) the cake using 300 g/10½ oz. of the buttercream. Chill in the fridge for 15 minutes.

Stir the vegan colouring into the remaining buttercream to achieve a mid-lilac shade (see colour tip). Use to coat the cake in a second layer of buttercream. Smooth and remove the excess. Press the flaked coconut onto the sides of the bottom third of the cake. Chill for 15 minutes.

Put the icing/confectioners' sugar in a bowl with the passion fruit pulp and seeds, and mix until smooth. Place spoonfuls on the top of the cake, allowing a little to trickle down the sides.

Thread two passion fruit halves onto the skewer and push into the cake. Decorate with the remaining passion fruit halves and pineapple leaves.

Colour tip
Playing around with purple! This is a mix of super food powders: mix ⅛ teaspoon pink pitaya powder and ⅛ teaspoon blue spirulina powder into the remaining 325 g/11½ oz. buttercream for the top coat to achieve this lilac-shade. Vegan gel and paste colourings are also available.

Pineapple & anise upside-down cake

The delicate and fragrant liquorice/licorice flavour of star anise takes this retro classic to a whole new level!

440-g/16-oz. can pineapple
  slices, drained, reserving
  2 tablespoons of the syrup
7 star anise
4 tablespoons maple syrup
2 tablespoons caster/superfine
  sugar
½ quantity of Vegan Deep
  Vanilla Sponge mixture
  (see page 15)
pineapple flowers, to decorate
  (optional, see decorating tip)
vegan ice-cream, to serve
  (optional)
23-cm/9-inch round, deep,
  spring-form cake pan,
  greased and lined
baking tray, lined with foil

Serves 10

Preheat the oven to 180°C (350°F) Gas 4.

Pat the pineapple rings with paper towels. Arrange six pineapple rings around the edge of the lined pan and one in the centre of the base of the pan. Place one star anise in the centre of each pineapple ring, pushing down so the star anise sits flush with the pineapple.

Put the reserved pineapple syrup in a pan with the maple syrup and caster/superfine sugar. Simmer, stirring, for 1 minute until the sugar has dissolved. Cool a little, then spoon over the pineapple in the pan.

Spoon the cake mixture over the pineapple slices and syrup. Level the surface. Put the cake pan on a baking tray lined with foil (just in case a small amount of the syrup leaks out). Bake in the preheated oven for 40–45 minutes until an inserted cocktail stick/toothpick comes out clean. Cool in the cake pan for 15 minutes.

Release the cake from the pan, trim the top to level if necessary, then invert onto a serving plate. Decorate with pineapple flowers, if liked. Serve warm or at room temperature with vegan ice-cream, if liked.

Decorating tip

For pineapple flowers, cut very thin slices (a large mandoline is good for this if you have one) from a peeled pineapple. Lay out onto paper towels, then use more paper towels to remove as much moisture as possible. Put the slices on a cooling rack over a baking tray. Dehydrate in the oven at around 100°C (200°F) Gas ¼ for 2–3 hours. When almost starting to crisp around the edges, allow to cool enough to handle, then place inside a mini muffin mould or the top of an espresso cup to take shape and fully dry out.

Epic Black Forest cake

Chocolate and cherry in all its glory! Brush each sponge layer with a little Kirsch to take this cake to even dizzier heights.

170 g/6 oz. dark/bittersweet vegan chocolate, broken into pieces

1 quantity of Vegan Chocolate Sponge mixture (see page 16), baked in three greased and lined 18-cm/7-inch cake pans for 30 minutes until an inserted cocktail stick/toothpick comes out clean, then cooled

1 quantity of Simple Vegan Vanilla Buttercream (see page 20)

50 g/2 oz. vegan black cherry conserve

150 g/5½ oz. fresh cherries

Serves 20

Lay two pieces of baking parchment, approximately 60 x 15 cm/ 24 x 6 inches, on the work surface in front of you.

Melt 140 g/5 oz. of the chocolate in a bain marie or in the microwave in 30-second bursts, stirring between each burst. Pour half the chocolate onto one piece of parchment in an elongated puddle and spread to approximately 50 x 12 cm/20 x 5 inches with a palette knife or metal spatula. Roll the parchment up from one of the shorter ends, so the chocolate only touches parchment. Place it seam-side down on a chopping board. Repeat with the rest of the chocolate and the second piece of parchment. Place in the fridge for 30 minutes, or until needed (it will keep for up to 2 days in the fridge like this).

Trim the tops of the cakes to make level if necessary. Sandwich together using 350 g/12½ oz. of the simple vegan vanilla buttercream and the cherry conserve – the bottom side of the top cake should be facing up. Place the cake on a cake board.

Crumb coat (see page 12) the cake using 450 g/1 lb. of the remaining buttercream. Place in the fridge for 15 minutes, then use the remaining buttercream to coat the cake in a second layer.

Unravel the chocolate parchment roll and stick the curled shards vertically to the sides of the cake.

Melt the remaining chocolate in a bain marie or in the microwave in 20-second bursts. Spread out the melted chocolate in the centre of the cake and use it to stick on the fresh cherries.

Strawberry shortcake layer cake

This recipe holds a little tasty tweak on those classic flavours by using my vegan 'mascarpone' cream. This not only tastes amazing but helps keep those sumptuous cakey layers in place.

320 g/generous 3 cups strawberries

1 quantity of Vegan Deep Vanilla Sponge mixture (see page 15), baked in 3 greased and lined 18-cm/7-inch cake pans for 30 minutes until an inserted cocktail stick/ toothpick comes out clean, then cooled

icing/confectioners' sugar, for dusting

'MASCARPONE' CREAM

400-g/14-oz. can coconut milk, chilled overnight (this helps separate the coconut cream from the water)

2 tablespoons cornflour/ cornstarch

2 tablespoons icing/ confectioners' sugar

170 g/³⁄₄ cup vegan cream cheese

Serves 20

To make the 'mascarpone' cream topping and filling, scoop out the hardened coconut cream and put it into a bowl, leaving behind the coconut water.

Mix 4 tablespoons of the coconut water with the cornflour/cornstarch to make a paste. Set aside.

Add the icing/confectioners' sugar to the bowl of coconut cream and mix with a hand-held electric whisk. Whisk the vegan cream cheese in a separate bowl to loosen, then whisk into the coconut cream mixture, a little at a time. Once combined, transfer the mixture to a small non-stick saucepan.

Heat over a medium heat, then, as the mixture begins to warm, add the cornflour/cornstarch paste. Stir frequently with a rubber spatula to prevent sticking until it begins to thicken. Once thick, cook for another minute to ensure the cornflour/cornstarch has cooked out. Transfer to a bowl. Cover with clingfilm/plastic wrap, making sure the clingfilm/plastic wrap touches the surface of the 'mascarpone' cream, then goes up the sides of the bowl – this will prevent a skin forming. Put it in the fridge to chill.

Once the 'mascarpone' is completely chilled, and you are ready to assemble the cake, hull and slice 175 g/1³⁄₄ cups of the strawberries. Leave the remainder whole or cut larger ones in half.

Trim the tops of the cakes to make level, if necessary. Place the base cake on a cake plate or serving board, spread with one-third of the 'mascarpone' cream and scatter over half of the sliced strawberries. Repeat with the next layer, using another third of the 'mascarpone' cream and the remaining sliced strawberries. Place the third sponge on top, spread with the remaining 'mascarpone' cream and top with the whole and halved strawberries. Dust with icing/confectioners' sugar.

Top tip

It's best to assemble this on the day of serving because of the fresh ingredients. Have all the components ready and it won't take long to assemble. Keep any leftovers chilled.

Knickerbocker glorious cake

Who doesn't love to dive into a sundae?! With a choc-chip and strawberry sponge, this is a guaranteed crowd pleaser!

100 g/3½ oz. dark/bittersweet vegan chocolate, chopped
7 g/¼ oz. freeze-dried strawberries
1 quantity of Vegan Deep Vanilla Sponge mixture (see page 15)

'FAN WAFERS'
½ quantity of Vegan Biscuit/Cookie Thins dough (see page 27)

TOPPING
1.050 kg/2 lb. 5 oz. Simple Vegan Vanilla Buttercream (see page 20) made using 350 g/12 oz. vegan butter and 700 g/5 cups icing/confectioners' sugar
300 g/10½ oz. white vegan chocolate
green, pink and blue food colouring (see tip page 11)
½–1 teaspoon coconut oil
a few tinned peach slices
1–2 strawberries, halved
vegan hundreds and thousands

CHOCOLATE SAUCE
25 g/3 tablespoons icing/confectioners' sugar
½ tablespoon unsweetened cocoa powder
1 tablespoon golden/light corn syrup
3 x 18-cm/7-inch cake pans, greased and lined
2 baking sheets, lined
piping/pastry bag

Serves 20

Preheat the oven to 180°C (350°F) Gas 4. Stir the chocolate and freeze-dried strawberries through the sponge mixture. Spoon into the cake pans and bake for 30 minutes until a cocktail stick/toothpick comes out clean. Cool in the pans for 10 minutes, then cool completely on wire racks.

Leave the oven on. For the 'fan wafers', roll out the dough between two pieces of baking parchment. Press the dough lightly with a floured potato masher to get a waffle pattern. Cut out 3 fan shapes, approximately 10 cm/4 inches long and 10 cm/4 inches at the widest point. Transfer to a lined baking sheet and chill for 15 minutes. Bake the biscuits/cookies for 20–25 minutes until golden. Cool on wire racks.

To make the 'ice-cream balls', cut 250 g/9 oz. from one of the three cakes, then crumble it using your fingertips to resemble breadcrumbs. Mix it with 125 g/4 oz. of the buttercream. Using slightly damp hands, roll into 7 equal-sized balls. Put them in the freezer for 20 minutes.

Melt 200 g/7 oz. of the white chocolate in a bowl over a pan of simmering water or in the microwave in 20-second bursts, stirring between each burst. One at a time, dip 2 of the balls in the white chocolate, turning to coat. Transfer to a lined baking sheet. Add green colouring to the chocolate and repeat with 2 or 3 more balls. Repeat with the remaining 100 g/3½ oz. of chocolate, the remaining balls and the pink colouring. If the chocolate starts to seize, add a little coconut oil. Chill until needed.

Reserve 300 g/10½ oz. of the buttercream, cover and set aside. Trim the tops of the 2 remaining cakes to make level. Sandwich the cakes together using 150 g/5 oz. of the buttercream. Place on a cake plate and crumb coat (see page 12) using 250 g/9 oz. of buttercream. Chill for 15 minutes.

Colour 350 g/12½ oz. of buttercream light blue and use to coat the cake in a second layer (apply with a dinner knife or palette knife/metal spatula to create lines in the buttercream – it doesn't need to be smooth).

Fill the piping/pastry bag with the reserved buttercream. Pipe 3 swirls on the base of the cake leaving space for the drippy ice cream balls. Pile up the ice cream balls with swirls of buttercream in-between.

Mix the chocolate sauce ingredients together with 1 teaspoon of water. It will be thick and sticky. Gradually add another ½–1 teaspoon of water until glossy with a pouring consistency. Drizzle over the cake. Decorate with hundreds and thousands, a 'fan wafer' and some strawberries.

Courgette/zucchini & lime cake

This unlikely but perfect pair get dressed up for their special loaf cake with a flourish of vibrant edible flowers!

125 g/4 oz. coarsely grated courgette/zucchini
grated zest of 2 limes
½ quantity of Vegan Deep Vanilla Sponge mixture (see page 15)

FILLING, FROSTING & DECORATION
grated zest of 2 limes

½ quantity Vegan Cream Cheese Frosting (see page 20)
3 courgette/zucchini flowers
10–15 small edible flowers
900-g/2-lb. loaf pan, greased and lined

Serves 10

Preheat the oven to 180°C (350°F) Gas 4.

Wrap the grated courgette/zucchini in paper towels and give it a good squeeze to remove as much water as possible. Repeat if necessary.

Fold the squeezed courgette/zucchini and lime zest through the sponge mixture, then spoon into the prepared loaf pan. Bake in the preheated oven for 60–65 minutes (cover loosely with foil after 45 minutes), until an inserted cocktail stick/toothpick comes out clean. Allow to cool in the pan for 10 minutes then remove and place on a wire rack to cool completely.

For the topping, stir the grated zest of 1 lime through the vegan cream cheese frosting before chilling, then chill it for 30 minutes. Spread onto the top of the cake. Decorate with zest from the remaining lime and the courgette/zucchini flowers and edible flowers. Chill the cake for at least 30 minutes, or until ready to serve.

Raspberry & nectarine crumble cake

Have your crumble and eat it! Dessert and cake in one – it doesn't get much better than this. The hardest part about this recipe is deciding whether to have it with vegan cream, ice-cream or a cup of tea.

315 g/scant 2$\frac{1}{2}$ cups plain/all-purpose flour
185 g/scant 1 cup caster/superfine sugar
3$\frac{1}{2}$ teaspoons baking powder
1$\frac{1}{4}$ teaspoons bicarbonate of soda/baking soda
1 teaspoon mixed/apple pie spice
320 g/1$\frac{1}{2}$ cups soya/soy yogurt
120 ml/$\frac{1}{2}$ cup sunflower oil
1$\frac{1}{2}$ tablespoons golden/light corn syrup
1 teaspoon pure vanilla extract

TOPPING
25 g/3 tablespoons plain/all-purpose flour
15 g/1 tablespoon vegan butter, cubed
15 g/1 tablespoon Demerara/raw sugar
25 g/scant $\frac{1}{4}$ cup hazelnuts, roughly chopped
2 ripe nectarines, stoned/pitted and cut into wedges
100 g/$\frac{3}{4}$ cup raspberries
whipped vegan cream or shop-bought vegan ice-cream, to serve (optional)
20-cm/8-inch spring-form deep cake pan, greased and lined

Serves 12

Preheat the oven to 180°C (350°F) Gas 4.

For the topping, put the flour, vegan butter and Demerara/raw sugar into a small bowl. Rub together with your fingertips until the mixture resembles fine breadcrumbs, then stir through the chopped hazelnuts. Set aside.

If the nectarines are very ripe, pat the wedges with paper towels.

For the cake batter, sift the flour into a large bowl, add the caster/superfine sugar, baking powder and bicarbonate of soda/baking soda, and mix with a spoon to combine. Make a well in the middle.

Put the soya/soy yogurt into a bowl and add the sunflower oil, golden/light corn syrup and vanilla extract. Mix with a spoon until fully combined. Pour into the well in the dry ingredients. Fold through with a spatula or wooden spoon until fully combined and smooth.

Spoon the cake mixture into the prepared cake pan and level the surface. Scatter the nectarines over the top, gently pushing them into the surface along with the raspberries. Top with the crumble mixture. Bake in the preheated oven for 45 minutes, then cover with foil and bake for a further 5–10 minutes until an inserted cocktail stick/toothpick comes out clean.

Cool in the pan for 10 minutes, then turn out of the pan and leave to cool completely on a wire rack, or serve warm with vegan whipped cream or vegan ice-cream.

Fab fault-line cake

Love your faults! That classic flavour combo gets a modern makeover!

finely grated zest of 2 oranges
1 quantity of Vegan Chocolate
   Sponge mixture
   (see page 16)
1 quantity of Simple Vegan
   Vanilla Buttercream
   (see page 20)
edible vegan gold paint
1 orange, for orange curls
25 g/1 oz. dark/bittersweet
   vegan chocolate, cut into
   shards directly from the bar

**DEHYDRATED
CANDIED ORANGE**
400 g/2 cups caster/superfine
   sugar
5 medium oranges, such as
   Cara or Navel, cut into
   3 mm/⅛ inch thick slices,
   seeds removed
2 baking sheets, lined
*3 x 18-cm/7-inch cake pans,
   greased and lined*
*disposable piping/pastry bag
   fitted with a 1-cm/½-inch
   round nozzle/tip*
wooden skewer

Serves 20

Preheat the oven to 120°C (250°F) Gas ½.

For the dehydrated candied orange, in a saucepan combine the sugar with 500 ml/2 cups of water. Bring to the boil over a medium-high heat, stirring until the sugar dissolves. Add the orange slices and simmer for 5–6 minutes. Use a slotted spoon to transfer the orange slices onto the lined baking sheets. Bake for 2 hours.

Leave to cool on a wire rack lined with parchment (they will become more rigid as they cool, but you still want them a little pliable).

For the cake, preheat the oven to 180°C (350°F) Gas 4.

Stir the finely grated orange zest through the sponge mix. Spoon into the cake pans. Bake for 30 minutes until an inserted cocktail stick/toothpick comes out clean. Leave to cool in the pans for 10 minutes, then transfer to wire racks to cool completely.

Trim the tops of the cakes to make level, if necessary. Reserve 100 g/3½ oz. of the buttercream, cover and set aside. Sandwich the cakes together using 350 g/12½ oz. of the plain buttercream – the bottom side of the top cake should be facing up. Place the cake on a cake plate or cake board.

Use 450 g/1 lb. of the plain buttercream to crumb coat the cake (see page 12). Gently press the candied orange slices around the middle of the cake. Chill for 30 minutes.

Spread the remaining buttercream generously around the base and top of the cake with a palette knife or metal spatula, ensuring it overlaps the oranges. Smooth with a palette knife, metal spatula or cake scraper. You will have little peaks around the top edge of the cake; using a palette knife or metal spatula, draw these inwards for a neat edge. Chill in the fridge for 1 hour.

Remove the cake from the fridge. Brush the edges of the fault line with the gold paint. Fill the piping/pastry bag with the reserved buttercream and pipe small peaks all around the top of the cake.

Pare the zest from the orange with a vegetable peeler. Cut into thin strips with a sharp knife or kitchen scissors, wrap around the skewer and squeeze a little to create a curl. Slice off-cuts into thin shorter pieces. Use to decorate the middle of the cake along with the chocolate shards.

Let's Go Nuts

Pistachio, lime & raspberry wowzer cake

Pistachios give this cake the most unbelievable taste and texture – working so well with the flavour pops of raspberry and zesty lime.

175 g/1¼ cups pistachio nuts, shelled
1 quantity of Vegan Deep Vanilla Sponge mixture (see page 15)
finely grated zest of 1 lime
4 tablespoons freeze-dried raspberries

DECORATION
1 quantity of Simple Vegan Vanilla Buttercream (see page 20), made with 400 g/14 oz. vegan butter, 2 teaspoons pure vanilla extract and 800 g/5¾ cups icing/confectioners' sugar
30 g/¼ cup raspberries, plus 5 to decorate
2 tablespoons vegan seedless raspberry or red berry jam/jelly
50 g/⅓ cup pistachio nuts, shelled and chopped
1–2 tablespoons freeze-dried raspberries
1–2 tablespoons pumpkin seeds
2 tablespoons pomegranate seeds
1–2 tablespoons goji berries
2 deep 20-cm/8-inch cake pans, greased and lined

Serves 20

Preheat the oven to 180°C (350°F) Gas 4.

For the cake, put the pistachio nuts in a food processor and blitz until finely chopped. Stir through the cake batter along with the lime zest and freeze-dried raspberries. Divide between the cake pans and bake in the preheated oven for 35 minutes until an inserted cocktail stick/toothpick comes out clean. Allow to cool in the pans for 10 minutes, then remove and place on a wire rack to cool completely.

Trim the tops from each cake to make level. Put 150 g/5½ oz. of the trimmings into a bowl (if you haven't got enough, shave a little from each cake until you have the correct amount of trimmings). Cover and set aside.

Sandwich the cakes together using 200 g/7 oz. of the buttercream – the bottom side of the top cake should be facing up. Place the cake on a cake board. Crumb coat (see page 12) the cake using 300 g/10½ oz. of the buttercream. Chill in the fridge for 15 minutes.

Use 300 g/10½ oz. of the remaining buttercream to coat the cake in a second layer of buttercream. Smooth and remove the excess.

Mash the raspberries to a pulp, then mix with the raspberry or red berry jam/jelly. Smear blobs of the jam/jelly mixture around the cake, then smooth and remove the excess to get a smooth two-tone effect.

Put the 150 g/5½ oz. of reserved cake trimmings into a bowl and break it up so it resembles breadcrumbs. Add 100 g/3½ oz. of the buttercream and mix with a fork until combined. Use like a 'clay' and press onto the cake to create a shawl-like shape. Chill in the fridge for 15 minutes.

Use a dinner knife to coat the 'shawl' roughly and very thickly using the remaining buttercream; this will cover it and act as a 'glue'. Stick on the chopped pistachio nuts, freeze-dried raspberries, pumpkin seeds, pomegranate seeds and goji berries. Use the 5 fresh raspberries to decorate the opposite side of the top of the cake.

Peanut butter & vegan jam/jelly

That salty, sweet match-made-in-heaven gets a cakey makeover!

1 quantity of Vegan Deep Vanilla Sponge mixture (see page 15) baked in 5 greased and lined 15-cm/6-inch cake pans (see equipment tip if you have only 2 pans) for 25–30 minutes until an inserted cocktail stick/toothpick comes out clean, then cooled

300 g/1 cup vegan strawberry jam/jelly

PEANUT BUTTER

600 g/4½ cups roasted salted peanuts, plus 1 tablespoon finely chopped peanuts to decorate (optional)

1 tablespoon golden/light corn syrup

100 ml/scant ½ cup vegetable oil, plus extra if needed

4–5 wooden skewers

Serves 20

Level four of the five cakes, if necessary. For the peanut butter, put the peanuts in a food processor with the golden/light corn syrup and blend until both crumbly and sticky – when it starts to stick to the sides, scrape it down. Start up the food processor and slowly add the oil with the motor running. Keep processing until smooth and thick, but with a good 'dropping' consistency. Add a little more oil if necessary.

Using a slightly off-set design, begin to sandwich the cakes together with dollops of the peanut butter and jam/jelly. After sandwiching together 3 layers, sturdy these base cakes by inserting 3 skewers (trimming to the height of the 3 cakes). Continue to place the remaining cakes on top, again sandwiching together with dollops of peanut butter and jam/jelly. Insert another 1 or 2 skewers, trimming to the full height of the cake. Scatter the top with finely chopped peanuts, if using.

Equipment tip

You may be more likely to have two cake pans rather than five! If so, spoon 280g/10 oz. of the cake mixture into one deep 15-cm/6-inch pan and bake for 25–30 minutes. Once the first mix has finished baking. Wash the tin and grease and re-line. Divide the remaining mix between this tin and a second deep 15-cm/6-inch greased and lined tin. Bake for 40 minutes. Allow to cool. Cut the two thicker cakes in half horizontally.

Marbled go nuts cupcakes

Get a caramel sweet and lightly spiced hit with these delicious nutty cake toppers. Placed on dreamy cashew buttercream with a light vanilla and nutty-chocolate base – this one is a nut-lovers paradise.

½ quantity of **Vegan Deep Vanilla Sponge mixture** (see page 15)

1 tablespoon good-quality **unsweetened cocoa powder,** mixed with 2 tablespoons just-boiled water

35 g/¼ cup **mixed nuts** (such as whole blanched almonds, pecans, cashews), chopped

½ **Cashew Nut Vanilla Frosting** (see page 23), chilled

CARAMEL SUGAR & SPICE NUTS

2 tablespoons **sugar**

1 teaspoon **ground cinnamon,** plus extra, for dusting

pinch **salt**

⅛ teaspoon mild **chilli/chili powder**

125 g/scant 1 cup **mixed nuts** (such as whole blanched almonds, pecans, cashews)

4 tablespoons **chickpea/garbanzo bean water**

baking tray, lined and sprayed with oil spray

12-hole muffin pan, lined with cases

disposable piping/pastry bag fitted with a 1.5-cm/½-inch round nozzle/tip

Makes 10–12

For the caramel sugar and spice nuts, preheat the oven to 150°C (300°F) Gas 1.

Put the sugar in a bowl with the cinnamon, salt and chilli/chili powder. Mix well. Add the mixed whole nuts.

Put the chickpea/garbanzo bean water into a bowl and beat with a hand-held electric whisk until frothy. Scoop up 2 tablespoons of the top froth and stir through the nut and sugar mixture to coat. Scatter over the lined and oiled baking sheet. Bake for 35 minutes, turning halfway, until browned. Allow to cool on the baking sheet.

For the cakes, preheat the oven to 180°C (350°F) Gas 4.

Divide the cake mixture between two bowls. Fold the cocoa powder mix, followed by the finely chopped nuts, through one bowl. Leave the second bowl plain.

Fill the cupcake cases with the cake batter, using alternate spoonfuls of the vanilla and nutty chocolate batter. Swirl with a cocktail stick/toothpick. Bake for 20–25 minutes until an inserted cocktail stick/toothpick comes out clean. Cool in the pan for 10 minutes, then place on a wire rack to cool completely.

Just before serving, fill the piping/pastry bag with the cashew nut vanilla frosting, twist the top of the bag and pipe a swirl on the top of each cake. Dust with a little cinnamon. Top each cake with the sugar and spice nuts.

Cherry bake 'wow' cake

An impressive 3-layer cake takes the understated cherry Bakewell to dizzy new heights. The addition of ground almonds in this cake batter, as well as cherry conserve in between its layers, give a delicious nod to one of my favourite guilty pleasures!

1 quantity of Vegan Deep Vanilla Sponge mixture (see page 15), swapping 100 g/¾ cup of the flour with 100 g/1 cup of ground almonds. Bake in 3 greased and lined 18-cm/ 7-inch cake pans for 30 minutes until an inserted cocktail stick/ toothpick comes out clean, then cooled
1 quantity of Simple Vegan Vanilla Buttercream (see page 20)
50 g/3 tablespoons vegan cherry conserve
pink vegan food colouring (optional, see colour tip)
35 g/scant ½ cup flaked/ sliced almonds
25 g/1 oz. vegan sugar pearls (optional)
7 vegan glacé cherries
disposable piping/pastry bag fitted with a 1D piping nozzle/tip

Serves 20

Trim the tops of the cakes to make level, if necessary. Sandwich together using 350 g/12 oz. of the buttercream and the cherry conserve – the bottom side of the top cake should be facing up. Place the cake on a cake plate or cake board.

Crumb coat (see page 12) the cake using 450 g/1 lb. of the remaining buttercream. Place in the fridge 15 minutes.

Put 150 g/5 oz. of the remaining buttercream into a bowl and set aside. Stir the pink vegan colouring through the remaining buttercream to make a 'baby pink' colour; use to coat the cake in a second layer. Smooth and remove the excess buttercream with a palette knife or metal spatula.

Gently press the flaked/sliced almonds onto the sides of the cake – covering about a quarter of the way up. Press the vegan pearls into the buttercream above this in a uniform line.

Place the reserved 150 g/5 oz. of buttercream into the piping/pastry bag and pipe seven little rosettes around the top edge of the cake. Top each with a glacé cherry.

Colour tip

There are now lots of vegan paste and gel colours available. However I used freeze-dried pink pitaya powder here. It's readily available online and a wonderfully natural way to achieve all shades of pink – use approximately ¾–1 teaspoon to get this baby pink shade – remember it darkens a little on standing.

Protein power squares

Increase your protein – in a cake! Packed with apricots and nuts and topped with protein power balls for a triple whammy!

25 g/scant ¼ cup blanched almonds, chopped
25 g/scant ¼ cup unsalted peanuts, toasted
35 g/¼ cup walnuts, chopped
50 g/⅓ cup dried apricots, chopped
grated zest of 1 orange
1 quantity of Vegan Terrific Traybake Sponge mixture (page 19)
50 g/2 oz. dark/bittersweet vegan chocolate, melted
50 g/2 oz. white vegan chocolate, melted

PROTEIN POWER BALLS
125 g/generous ½ cup thick smooth peanut butter
1½ tablespoons golden/light corn syrup
120 g/⅔ cup cooked quinoa
40 g/generous ½ cup pumpkin seeds, plus extra for decorating
unsweetened cocoa powder, for dusting
20 x 30-cm/8 x 12-inch pan, greased and lined

Serves 15

Preheat the oven to 180°C (350°F) Gas 4.

Gently fold the chopped nuts, apricots and orange zest through the batter. Spoon into the prepared cake pan. Bake in the preheated oven for 35–40 minutes. Allow to cool in the pan for 10 minutes. Carefully invert onto a chopping board to remove from the pan, then invert again onto a cooling rack to cool completely.

Meanwhile, make the protein power balls. Whiz all the ingredients in a food processor until smooth and sticky. Roll the mixture into 15 balls. Roll each in the cocoa powder and decorate with a pumpkin seed.

Drizzle the melted chocolate over the cooled cake. Top with the protein power balls. Leave to set, then cut into 15 squares.

Carrot cake with cashew nut frosting

Carrot ribbons and striking caramel shards ramp up the style-stakes in this favourite.

315 g/scant 2½ cups
  plain/all-purpose flour
185 g/scant 1 cup caster/
  superfine sugar
3½ teaspoons baking powder
1¼ teaspoons bicarbonate
  of soda/baking soda
2 teaspoons mixed/
  apple pie spice
320 g/1½ cups soya/
  soy yogurt
120 ml/½ cup sunflower oil
1½ tablespoons golden/
  light corn syrup
1 teaspoon pure vanilla
  extract
200 g/7 oz. carrot, peeled
  and grated
100 g/scant 1 cup roughly
  chopped walnuts
40 g/scant ⅓ cup sultanas/
  golden raisins

**FILLING, FROSTING
& DECORATION**
1 large carrot
400 g/2 cups caster/superfine
  sugar
½ quantity of Cashew Nut
  Vanilla Frosting
  (see page 23)
50 g/scant ½ cup roughly
  chopped walnuts, plus
  10–12 walnut halves
  to decorate
2 baking sheets, 1 lined, 1 oiled
*2 deep 20-cm/8-inch cake pans,
  greased and lined*
*disposable piping/pastry bag,
  with the tip cut to make
  a 2.5-cm/1-inch hole*

Serves 12

Start by making the carrot curls for decoration. Preheat the oven to 100°C (200°F) Gas ¼. Cut the carrot into ribbons using a vegetable peeler. In a saucepan combine 200 g/1 cup of the sugar with 200 ml/scant 1 cup of water. Bring to the boil over a medium-high heat, stirring until the sugar dissolves. Add the carrot ribbons and simmer for 5–6 minutes. Use a slotted spoon to remove, then, when cool enough to handle, place in flat strips on the lined baking sheet.

Bake in the preheated oven for 30–45 minutes until they are dehydrated but still flexible, then remove from the oven and, working quickly, wrap around wooden spoon handles and set aside to dry out fully; around 30 minutes.

Increase the oven temperature to 180°C (350°F) Gas 4 for the cake. Sift the flour into a large bowl, add the sugar, baking powder, bicarbonate of soda/baking soda and mixed/apple pie spice, and mix with a spoon to combine. Make a well in the middle.

Put the yogurt into a bowl and add the sunflower oil, golden/light corn syrup and vanilla extract. Mix with a spoon until fully combined. Pour into the well of dry ingredients. Fold through with a spatula or wooden spoon until combined and smooth. Fold through the remaining cake ingredients.

Transfer to the greased and lined pans. Bake for 35 minutes until an inserted cocktail stick/toothpick comes out clean. Leave to cool in the pans for 10 minutes, then transfer to wire racks to cool completely.

For the caramel shards, put the remaining 200 g/1 cup sugar in a saucepan and cook over a medium heat, without stirring (swirl the pan a little if necessary), until the sugar melts and turns a golden colour. Pour onto the oiled baking sheet. Leave to cool and set. Roughly break into decorative shards. Set aside.

Mix half of the cashew nut frosting with the chopped walnuts and use to sandwich the cakes together. Fill the piping/pastry bag with the remaining frosting and use to pipe blobs of the cashew nut frosting around the top edge and centre of the cake. Insert caramel shards into the top and decorate with the carrot curls and walnut halves.

Hello Petal

Orange blossom semolina cake with rhubarb drizzle

I love this pairing, not only for the harmonious flavour combination, but for these completely natural colour-clashing brights simply doing their thang on the cakey stage!

2 oranges, thinly sliced
grated zest of 2 oranges
½ quantity of Vegan Deep Vanilla Sponge mixture (see page 15), replacing the flour with 140g/scant 1½ cups ground almonds and 100g/⅔ cup fine semolina)

ORANGE SYRUP
125 ml/½ cup orange juice
1 tablespoon orange blossom water
60 g/generous ¼ cup caster/superfine sugar

RHUBARB DRIZZLE
225 g/8 oz. rhubarb
60 g/generous ¼ cup caster/superfine sugar
2 tablespoons fresh orange juice
20-cm/8-inch spring-form cake pan, greased and lined

Serves 10

Preheat the oven to 180°C (350°F) Gas 4.

Prepare the syrup, put the orange juice in a saucepan with the orange blossom water and caster/superfine sugar. Simmer for 8–10 minutes until reduced and thickened slightly. Allow to cool a little.

For the cake, arrange the orange slices in the bottom of the cake pan. Drizzle over 5 tablespoons of the syrup. Set aside the remaining syrup.

Fold the orange zest through the sponge mixture, then spoon into the prepared pan over the top of the orange slices. Bake in the preheated oven for 45–50 minutes (put a baking tray on the shelf beneath to catch any small drips from the orange syrup.

Meanwhile, make the rhubarb drizzle. Put the rhubarb and sugar in a saucepan with the orange juice. Gently heat until the rhubarb begins to release its juices. Bring to a simmer and cook for 10 minutes until the rhubarb is tender. Allow to cool to room temperature. Blitz in a mini food processor until smooth. Allow to cool.

Allow the cake to cool in the pan for 10 minutes, then remove the sides of the tin. Carefully invert onto a cooling rack, then carefully remove the base (now the top) of the tin, revealing the orange slices.

Brush with the remaining syrup. Serve warm or at room temperature. Spoon over the rhubarb drizzle just before serving. Serve any extra rhubarb drizzle on the side for extra spoonfuls on servings, if liked.

Blueberry & lavender cake

With such a zingy, refreshing flavour this zesty little number
almost feels like a healthier cake option… I did say, almost!

325 g/1½ cups plus
   2 tablespoons caster/
   superfine sugar
3 teaspoons dried lavender
   buds
400 g/3 cups blueberries,
   plus 75 g/generous
   ½ cup for decoration
freshly squeezed juice
   of ½ lemon
1 quantity of Vegan Deep
   Vanilla Sponge mixture
   (see page 15), baked in
   2 greased and lined deep
   20-cm/8-inch cake pans
   for 30–35 minutes until
   an inserted cocktail stick/
   toothpick comes out
   clean, then cooled
1 quantity of Vegan Cream
   Cheese Frosting
   (see page 20)
6–8 blackberries
1 tablespoon golden/
   light corn syrup
edible or food-safe flowers
   (optional)
icing/confectioners' sugar,
   for dusting

Serves 20

Put 75 g/¼ cup plus 2 tablespoons of the caster/superfine
sugar into a pan with 125 ml/½ cup of water and the
lavender buds. Place the pan on a medium heat and allow
to bubble until the sugar has dissolved and the liquid has
reduced slightly. Strain through a fine sieve/strainer.
Discard the buds and allow the liquid to cool.

Put the blueberries, lemon juice and the remaining
250 g/1¼ cups of sugar in a medium pan. Bring to the boil,
then simmer for 20–25 minutes until thickened, stirring
frequently. Allow to cool to room temperature, then use
straight away or chill in the fridge until needed.

Trim one cake so it is level, then cut horizontally through
the middle of each so you have 4 layers. Brush the lavender
syrup over the cut sides of the sponges (they only need
a very light brushing – about 1 tablespoon on each layer).

Set aside 3 tablespoons of the cream cheese frosting, and
use the remainder to sandwich the cakes together with
the blueberry compote (see decorating tip). With a dinner
knife, smear a crescent shape using the reserved cream
cheese frosting to one side of the top. Decorate with the
extra blueberries and the blackberries. Use the golden/light
corn syrup to help stick and build up the berries – an extra
drizzle at the end doesn't hurt either! Add edible/food-safe
flowers, if using. Chill the cake for at least 30 minutes, or
until ready to serve. Dust with icing/confectioners' sugar
just before serving.

Top tip

With the gorgeous moist sponge and deep vibrant sticky
compote, the colour absorbs into the sponge. To keep
this cake looking its best, it works best putting the cream
cheese frosting layer first. I love this dramatic taste and
effect, but I would assemble and serve on the same day!

Elderflower & lemon cakes

Step into Spring with these cute little cakes; zesty with a delicate floral touch. Perfect as part of an afternoon tea.

finely grated zest of 2 lemons
½ quantity of Vegan Deep Vanilla Sponge mixture (see page 15)
freshly squeezed juice of 1 lemon
6 tablespoons elderflower cordial
5–6 tablespoons caster/superfine sugar
fresh edible flowers, to decorate
20-cm/8-inch square loose-bottomed cake pan, greased and lined

Makes 16

Preheat the oven to 180°C (350°F) Gas 4.

Stir the finely grated lemon zest through the sponge mix. Spoon into the cake pan. Bake for 30–35 minutes until an inserted cocktail stick/toothpick comes out clean. Leave to cool in the pan for 10 minutes.

Stir the lemon juice through the cordial. Prick the cake all over using a cocktail stick/toothpick. Drizzle over the elderflower and lemon syrup, then sprinkle over the sugar. Leave to cool completely, then remove from the pan. Trim the sides of the cake with a sharp serrated knife, then cut into 16 equal squares. Decorate with edible flowers.

Rose petal chocolate cake

A real crowd-pleaser and no one will know how simple it is. You can even freeze the sponges ahead of time, assemble and ice them the day before, and simply top with a scattering of rose petals on the day!

1 quantity of Vegan Chocolate Sponge mixture (see page 16), baked in two greased and lined 20-cm/8-inch cake pans for 35 minutes until an inserted cocktail stick/toothpick comes out clean, then cooled
1 quantity of Vegan Chocolate Fudge Icing (see page 23)
3 food-safe roses (colour of your choice)

Serves 20

Trim the cakes so they are level, if necessary, then cut horizontally through the middle of each so you have four layers.

Sandwich together with 400 g/14 oz. vegan chocolate fudge icing – the bottom side of the top cake should be facing up.

Generously coat the cake in the remaining icing using large sweeping motions with a butter knife, small palette knife or metal spatula.

Decorate with 2 of the roses and a scattering of petals from the remaining rose.

Turkish delights

Shop-bought Turkish delight may contain gelatine, but this recipe includes homemade vegan versions. Always read the label if you want to use shop-bought ones instead.

1 teaspoon rose water
½ quantity of Vegan Deep
    Vanilla Sponge mixture
    (see page 15)
60 g/generous ⅓ cup
    pistachio nuts, chopped
vegan peach food colouring
    (optional, see page 11)
¼ quantity of Simple Vegan
    Vanilla Buttercream
    (see page 20)
2 teaspoons freeze-dried
    rose petals
10–20 mint leaves, to decorate

TURKISH DELIGHT
400 g/2 cups caster/
    superfine sugar
½ tablespoon freshly
    squeezed lemon juice
½ teaspoon cream of tartar
65 g/⅔ cup cornflour/
    cornstarch
½ tablespoon rose water
vegan pink paste or gel
    food colouring (optional,
    see page 11)
icing/confectioners' sugar,
    for dusting
sugar thermometer (optional)
15-cm/6-inch square cake pan,
    greased and lined (also grease
    the top of the parchment
    with a touch of oil)
12-hole muffin pan, lined
    with cases
piping/pastry bag fitted
    with a 2D nozzle/tip

Makes 10–12

For the Turkish delight, put the sugar, lemon juice and 185 ml/¾ cup of water into a small–medium saucepan over a medium heat and stir until the sugar has dissolved. Bring to the boil and continue to boil, stirring, until it reaches 115°C/240°F. (If you are not using a sugar thermometer, test the syrup by dropping a teaspoonful into a glass of cold water. If it forms a soft ball, the syrup is ready.) It should take 10–15 minutes to reach this stage. The syrup will be a light amber colour. Set aside to cool.

While the syrup is cooling, put 250 ml/1 cup of water into another small–medium saucepan with the cream of tartar and the cornflour/cornstarch. Place over a medium heat, whisking continuously to avoid lumps, until you have a very thick paste.

Carefully, pour the syrup into the cornflour/cornstarch paste, a little at a time, whilst whisking. Once you've added in all the syrup, whisk a little more to ensure you have a smooth, golden, semi-translucent paste.

Bring the paste to the boil, then turn the heat down to the lowest setting on the smallest hob ring/stove top burner and simmer gently for around 1 hour until it is a deep golden colour, stirring every few minutes to prevent sticking. Remove from the heat and stir in the rose water and food colouring (if using).

Pour into the prepared cake pan and give it a bit of a shake to ensure the mixture gets to the corners. Cover with a piece of lightly oiled baking parchment. Leave for 5–6 hours or overnight to set. (You won't need it all for the cakes – enjoy the remainder as a little sweet treat with herbal tea. Store in an airtight container in a cool dry place for up to 1 month.)

For the cakes, preheat the oven to 180°C (350°F) Gas 4.

Add the rose water to the sponge mixture and stir through 50 g/⅓ cup of the pistachio nuts, then divide the mixture between the cases and bake in the preheated oven for 25 minutes, until an inserted cocktail stick/toothpick comes out clean. Allow to cool in the muffin pan for 10 minutes, then remove and place on a wire rack to cool completely.

Add a little peach colouring to the buttercream, if liked. Fill the piping/pastry bag with the buttercream, twist the top and pipe a swirl on each cake, slightly to one side, to resemble a rose. On the opposite side, pipe 3–4 little stars. Scatter with freeze-dried rose petals and the remaining pistachio nuts. Finish with a mint leaf and a piece of Turkish delight.

Forget-me-not Prosecco jelly cake

Grown up jelly? Yes please! Edible flowers frozen in time in a delectable
Prosecco jelly dome on top of a two-layer chocolate and vanilla cake.

315 g/scant 2½ cups plain/
  all-purpose flour
185 g/scant 1 cup caster/superfine
  sugar
3½ teaspoons baking powder
1¼ teaspoons bicarbonate of
  soda/baking soda
320 g/1½ cups soya/soy yogurt
120 ml/½ cup sunflower oil
1½ tablespoons golden/light
  corn syrup
1 teaspoon pure vanilla extract
1½ tablespoons good-quality
  unsweetened cocoa powder
  mixed with 2½ tablespoons
  just-boiled water
450 g/1 lb. Simple Vegan Vanilla
  Buttercream (see page 20) made
  with 150 g/5 oz. vegan butter
  and 300 g/generous 2 cups
  icing/confectioners' sugar

JELLY/JELLO
3–5 large edible/food-safe flowers, a
  few petals removed and reserved
25–30 small edible/food-safe flowers
few sprigs of rosemary (optional)
450 ml/scant 2 cups Prosecco
100 ml/scant ½ cup elderflower
  cordial
4 x 6.5-g/¼-oz. sachets vege gel
400-ml/14-oz. can coconut milk
3 tablespoons icing/confectioners'
  sugar

SIDES
150 g/5 oz. dark/bittersweet vegan
  chocolate, broken into pieces
2-litre/2-quart Pyrex dish
*2 x 18-cm/7-inch loose-bottomed
  cake pans, greased and lined*

Serves 12

For the jelly/jello, put the flowers and rosemary in the base of the
Pyrex dish. Put the Prosecco and elderflower cordial in a saucepan,
sprinkle over 2 of the vege gel sachets, stir until dissolved, then
place over a medium heat and bring slowly to the boil while
stirring. Simmer for 5 minutes, stirring all the time. Pour over the
flowers. Some will float to the surface; you can ease them around
the sides and push them down a little with the end of a spoon as
it sets, but work quickly and transfer it to the fridge within a few
minutes, or it may become mushy. Chill for 2–3 hours.

Put the coconut milk in a saucepan and whisk until smooth. Whisk
in the icing/confectioners' sugar. Sprinkle over the remaining vege
gel sachets, stir until dissolved, then place over a medium heat and
heat as before. After 5 minutes simmering, remove from the heat.
Continue to whisk for 20–30 seconds, then gently, but working
quickly, pour over the Prosecco base. Chill for 3–4 hours.

Preheat the oven to 180°C (350°F) Gas 4. Sift the flour into a bowl,
add the sugar, baking powder and bicarbonate of soda/baking soda
and mix to combine. Make a well in the middle. Put the yogurt into
a bowl and mix in the sunflower oil, syrup and vanilla. Pour into
the well of dry ingredients and fold until just smooth. Divide the
mix between two bowls. Fold the cocoa powder mix through one
bowl. Spoon into the cake pans. Bake for 30–35 minutes until an
inserted cocktail stick/toothpick comes out clean. Cool in the pans
for 10 minutes, then cool completely on wire racks.

Trim the tops of the cakes to make level, if necessary. With
the vanilla cake as the base, sandwich the cakes together using
150 g/5 oz. of the buttercream. Place on a cake plate. Crumb
coat (see page 12) the cakes using the remaining buttercream.

For the sides, make chocolate shards following the method on
page 39, rolling the parchment a little looser for wider shards.

Invert the jelly onto one of the cake pan bases. If the jelly does not
come out first time, dip in a large bowl of hot water for 10 seconds.

Slide the jelly on top of the cake. Press the chocolate shards onto
the side of the cake. If the buttercream on the sides has crusted
over a little, very lightly brush with a little water.

Pumpkin Persian love cake

Persian love cake has been given the va va voom touch in this two layer version
and of course these mini dried roses were crying out to be scattered over the top!

215 g/generous 1½ cups plain/
   all-purpose flour
100 g/1 cup ground almonds
1 teaspoon cinnamon
½ teaspoon grated nutmeg
5 cardamom pods, peeled, seeds crushed
185 g/scant 1 cup caster/superfine sugar
3½ teaspoons baking powder
1¼ teaspoons bicarbonate of soda/
   baking soda
320 g/1½ cups soya/soy yogurt
120 ml/½ cup sunflower oil
1½ tablespoons golden/light corn syrup
2½ tablespoons rose water
175 g/6 oz. freshly grated butternut
   squash
1 teaspoon almond extract

FILLING
450 g/1 lb. Simple Vegan Vanilla
   Buttercream (see page 20) made
   with 150 g/5 oz. vegan butter, 300 g/
   generous 2 cups icing/confectioners'
   sugar, and 2 teaspoons rose water
   instead of water
vegan green and pink food colouring
   (optional, see page 11)

TOPPING & DECORATION
1 quantity of Vegan Royal Icing
   (see page 24)
2 teaspoons rose water
7–10 small dried roses
1 teaspoon dried rose petals
15 g/½ oz. pistachio nuts, chopped
*2 x 18-cm/7-inch cake pans, greased
   and lined*
*1 disposable piping/pastry bag,
   fitted with a closed star nozzle/tip*
*1 disposable piping/pastry bag,
   fitted with an open star nozzle/tip*

Serves 12

Preheat the oven to 180°C (350°F) Gas 4.

Sift the flour into a large bowl, add the ground almonds, cinnamon, nutmeg, cardamom, sugar, baking powder and bicarbonate of soda/baking soda, and mix with a spoon. Make a well in the middle.

Put the soya/soy yogurt into a blender with the sunflower oil, golden/light corn syrup, rose water, butternut squash and almond extract. Pulse and blend until smooth. Pour into the well of dry ingredients. Fold through with a spatula or wooden spoon until just combined and smooth. Transfer to the greased and lined pan. Bake for 45 minutes, then cover loosely with a square of baking parchment and bake for another 10 minutes, until an inserted cocktail stick/toothpick comes out clean. Leave to cool in the pan for 10 minutes, then transfer to a wire rack to cool completely.

For the filling, divide the buttercream between two bowls. Colour one bowl pink and one green (if colouring). Fill the piping/pastry bag fitted with the closed star nozzle/tip with the pink buttercream and the piping/pastry bag fitted with open star nozzle/tip with the green.

Place one cake on a cake plate or cake board. Starting with one colour, pipe blobs around the edge of the cake, leaving gaps for the other colour. Continue inwards in circles until completely covered (except for the gaps left for the second colour). Use the second colour to fill the gaps.

Place the second cake on top. Stir the rose water through the royal icing. Add a little more icing/confectioners' sugar if this makes it a little too loose; you want it to thickly coat the back of a spoon.

Spoon the icing on top of the cake. It's best to tip several smaller spoonfuls over the cake and let them join up and drizzle, rather than try to spread the icing, as this will pick up the crumbs beneath. Scatter over the dried roses, dried rose petals and pistachio nuts.

Chocs Away

Squishiest ever chocolate cake!

Just when you thought vegan chocolate cake couldn't get better...

300 g/10½ oz. vegan brownies (shop-bought or ½ quantity of Indulgent Chocolate Chip Brownie mixture, see page 88, baked in a 15-cm/6-inch square lined pan for 25–30 minutes, then cooled; see Top tip)

½ quantity of Vegan Chocolate Fudge Icing (see page 23)

225 g/8 oz. Simple Vegan Vanilla Buttercream (see page 20) made with 75 g/¾ stick butter and 150 g/1 cup icing/confectioners' sugar, and 1 tablespoon cocoa powder mixed with 2 tablespoons just-boiled water instead of the water

315 g/scant 2½ cups plain/all-purpose flour

3½ tablespoons good-quality unsweetened cocoa powder

185 g/scant 1 cup caster/superfine sugar

3½ teaspoons baking powder

1¼ teaspoons bicarbonate of soda/baking soda

320 g/1½ cups soya/soy yogurt

120 ml/½ cup sunflower oil

1½ tablespoons golden/light corn syrup

vegan edible gold spray and edible gold leaf, to decorate (optional)

2 x 18-cm/7-inch cake pans, greased and lined

Serves 12

Preheat the oven to 180°C (350°F) Gas 4.

Break the brownies into pieces. Put most of the brownie pieces into a large bowl with half the chocolate fudge icing and the chocolate vegan buttercream. Mix gently, allowing it to marble. Try not to mix too much, as the separate colours and textures work really well.

Sift the flour into a large bowl, add the cocoa powder, caster/superfine sugar, baking powder and bicarbonate of soda/baking soda, and mix with a spoon to combine. Make a well in the middle.

Put the soya/soy yogurt into a bowl, add the sunflower oil and golden/light corn syrup. Mix with a spoon until fully combined. Pour into the well of dry ingredients. Fold through with a spatula or wooden spoon until just combined and just smooth. Transfer to the greased and lined pans and bake for 30–35 minutes.

Trim the tops of both cakes to make level. Place one cake on a serving platter or cake plate. Top with the brownie mixture and place the second cake on top, flat-side facing upwards.

Use a dinner knife or small palette knife to cover the top of the cake with the remaining fudge icing. Spray with the gold spray, if using. Top with the remaining brownies and the edible gold leaf, if using.

Top tip

This will give you around 650 g/1 lb. 7 oz. of cooked brownies – you can always freeze the remainder. Wrap in clingfilm/plastic wrap and freeze for up to 3 months. Allow to defrost at room temperature.

Chocolate & salted caramel chickpea cake

What do you do with the chickpeas/garbanzo beans after making meringue? Add them to a cake for a dense, luxurious texture with a delicious nutty flavour. Coated in chocolate fudge icing and salted caramel, chickpeas/garbanzo beans have never looked so sexy!

400-g/14-oz. can chickpeas/
  garbanzo beans, drained
320 g/1½ cups soya/soy yogurt,
  plus 2 tablespoons
275 g/2 cups plain/all-purpose
  flour
3½ tablespoons cocoa powder
185 g/scant 1 cup caster/
  superfine sugar
3½ teaspoons baking powder
1¼ teaspoons bicarbonate
  of soda/baking soda
½–1 teaspoon salt
120 ml/½ cup sunflower oil
2½ tablespoons golden/light
  corn syrup
2 teaspoons pure vanilla extract

FROSTING & TOPPING
½ quantity of Vegan Chocolate
  Fudge Icing (see page 23)
1 quantity of Soft Vegan Caramel
  Sauce (see page 24), with
  up to 1 teaspoon sea salt
  (to taste) stirred through
  with the melted coconut oil

DECORATION
100 g/3½ oz. dark/bittersweet
  vegan chocolate, chopped
100 g/3½ oz. milk vegan
  chocolate, chopped
pink rock salt or rock salt
2 x 18-cm/7-inch cake pans,
  greased and lined
2 baking sheets, lined

Serves 12

Preheat the oven to 180°C (350°F) Gas 4.

Purée the chickpeas/garbanzo beans in a blender or food processor with the 2 tablespoons soya/soy yogurt. Set aside.

Sift the flour into a large bowl, add the cocoa powder, caster/superfine sugar, baking powder, bicarbonate of soda/baking soda and salt, and mix with a spoon to combine. Make a well in the middle.

Put the remaining soya/soy yogurt into a bowl, add the sunflower oil, golden/light corn syrup and vanilla extract. Mix with a spoon until fully combined. Pour into the well of dry ingredients. Fold through with a spatula or wooden spoon until just combined and smooth. Fold through the puréed chickpeas/garbanzo beans. Transfer to the greased and lined pans. Bake for 30–35 minutes until an inserted cocktail stick/toothpick comes out clean.

Trim the tops of the cakes to make level if necessary. Sandwich the cakes together using 150 g/5 oz. of the chocolate fudge icing – the bottom side of the top cake should be facing up. Place the cake on a cake plate or cake board.

Coat the cake using the remaining icing. Smooth with a palette knife, metal spatula or cake scraper.

Meanwhile make the chocolate brush marks to decorate. Melt each of the chocolates separately in a bowl set over a pan of simmering water or in the microwave in 20-second bursts, stirring between each burst. Dip a pastry brush into the dark chocolate and brush thick brush marks onto the parchment-lined baking sheets. Scatter over the salt. Clean the brush and repeat with the milk chocolate. Chill in the fridge to set.

Pour the soft caramel sauce around the top of the cake, next to the edge, allowing it to trickle down the sides, then work in a spiral motion moving inwards to completely cover the top of the cake. Sweep across the top with a long palette knife/metal spatula to smooth.

Insert the salted chocolate pieces into the top of the cake.

Oreo cookie cake

Not quite vegan? Join the debate... Although the ingredients in Oreos are vegan, they may have cross-contact with milk, so strictly speaking they're not. Some people who do their best to live a plant-based diet say when in need of an accessible chocolaty treat, they're a good option – this cake is for those in that camp!

1 quantity of **Vegan Chocolate Sponge** (see page 16), baked in 3 greased and lined 18-cm/7-inch cake pans for 30 minutes until an inserted cocktail stick/toothpick comes out clean, then cooled

1 quantity of **Simple Vegan Vanilla Buttercream** (see page 20)

60 g/2¼ oz. Oreo cookies (approx. 6 cookies), plus 8–10 cookies, to decorate

100 g/3½ oz. dark/bittersweet vegan chocolate, melted

disposable piping/pastry bag fitted with a 2D nozzle/tip

Serves 20

Trim the tops of the cakes to make level if necessary. Sandwich together using 350 g/12 oz. of the simple vegan buttercream – the bottom side of the top cake should be facing up. Place the cake on a cake plate or board.

Crumb coat (see page 12) the cake using 450 g/1 lb. of the remaining buttercream. Place in the fridge 15 minutes. Put 150 g/5 oz. of the buttercream in a bowl, cover and set aside.

Put the Oreos in a food processor and whiz to fine crumbs. Set aside 4 tablespoons, then stir the rest of the crumbs through the remaining buttercream and use to coat the cake in a second layer, smoothing with a palette knife, metal spatula or cake scraper. Chill for 15 minutes.

Pour the melted chocolate around the top of the cake, next to the edge, allowing it to trickle down the sides, then work in a spiral motion moving inwards to completely cover the top of the cake. Sweep across the top with a long palette knife or metal spatula to smooth. Chill for 30 minutes.

Put the reserved buttercream into the piping/pastry bag. Pipe 8–10 little rosettes around the top of the cake. Insert an Oreo into each rosette. Press the reserved crumbs around the bottom of the cake.

Indulgent chocolate chip brownies

The best-dressed brownie goes to... ok, so the edible gold is entirely optional, but eating one of these rich, moist brownies is a must! Cook for slightly less time for the ultimate gooey brownie or cook a little longer if you prefer a firmer texture.

250 g/scant 2 cups plain/
  all-purpose flour, sifted
75 g/¾ cup unsweetened
  cocoa powder
1 teaspoon baking powder
200 g/1 cup caster/superfine
  sugar
125 g/generous ½ cup light
  soft brown sugar
75 g/generous ¼ cup dark
  soft brown sugar
1 tablespoon instant coffee
  granules
250 g/9 oz. vegan butter,
  melted
1 teaspoon pure vanilla
  extract
275 g/scant 1¼ cups soya/
  soy yogurt
275 g/10 oz. dark/bittersweet
  vegan chocolate
edible gold leaf (optional)
20 x 30-cm/8 x 12-inch baking
  pan, greased and lined

Serves 15

Preheat the oven to 180°C (350°F) Gas 4.

Put the flour in a large bowl with the cocoa powder, baking powder, caster/superfine sugar, light brown sugar, dark brown sugar and instant coffee. Mix well to combine and create a well in the middle.

Add the melted vegan butter, vanilla extract and soya/soy yogurt to the well, and mix well with a wooden spoon or spatula to combine.

Melt 100 g/3½ oz. of the dark/bittersweet vegan chocolate in a bain marie or in the microwave in 20-second bursts, stirring in-between each burst. Add to the batter and use a hand-held electric whisk to mix. Cut the remaining chocolate into smallish chunks, and stir most through the batter.

Spoon into the prepared pan and level the surface. Scatter over the remaining chunks of chocolate. Bake in the preheated oven for 35–40 minutes until an inserted cocktail stick/toothpick comes out clean around the edges – you still want it to be a little sticky in the middle for gooey brownies.

Remove from the oven and allow to cool completely in the pan on a wire rack. Turn out and cut into 15 squares.

Red velvet cake

Keeping with tradition, I'm using beetroot/beets for the red hue in this much-loved cake. When foods were rationed in World War II bakers used boiled beetroot/beet juices to enhance the colour of their cakes, it also acted as a filler (making this cake even bigger!). Using 21st-century equipment I found whizzing raw beetroot/beets in a blender a great short-cut! Bring on the beetroot/beets!

480 g/3²/₃ cups plain/
   all-purpose flour
4 tablespoons unsweetened
   cocoa powder
280 g/scant 1½ cups caster/
   superfine sugar
5 teaspoons baking powder
1½ teaspoons bicarbonate
   of soda/baking soda
480 g/2¼ cups soya/soy
   yogurt
180 ml/¾ cup sunflower oil
2 tablespoons golden/
   light corn syrup
275 g/10 oz. freshly grated
   beetroot/beets
2 tablespoons freshly
   squeezed lemon juice

FROSTING
345 g/12 oz. vegan butter
690 g/5 cups icing/
   confectioners' sugar
115 g/4 oz. vegan cream
   cheese

DECORATION
1 beetroot/beet
½ tablespoon vegetable oil
*2 baking sheets, greased
   and lined*
*3 x 18-cm/7-inch cake pans,
   greased and lined*

Serves 20

Preheat the oven to 120°C (250°F) Gas ½.

For the beetroot/beet crisp decoration, cut the beetroot/beet into thin slices using a mandoline. Toss in the vegetable oil to coat (see top tip).

Transfer to the lined baking sheets. Bake for 1 hour until crisp – they will crisp more on cooling. Slide the parchment onto cooling racks to cool.

Preheat the oven to 180°C (350°F) Gas 4.

Sift the flour into a large bowl, add the cocoa powder, caster/superfine sugar, baking powder and bicarbonate of soda/baking soda, and mix with a spoon to combine. Make a well in the middle.

Put the soya/soy yogurt into a blender with the sunflower oil, golden/light corn syrup, beetroot/beets and lemon juice. Pulse and blend until smooth. Pour into the well of dry ingredients. Fold through with a spatula or wooden spoon until just combined and smooth.

Transfer to the greased and lined pans and bake for 30–35 minutes until an inserted cocktail stick/toothpick comes out clean. Leave to cool in the pans for 10 minutes, then transfer to wire racks to cool completely.

For the frosting, place the vegan butter, icing/confectioners' sugar and cream cheese in a food processor and pulse until blended.

Trim the tops of the cakes to make level (reserve at least 40 g/1½ oz. of the trimmings). Halve the cakes horizontally. Sandwich together using 375 g/13 oz. of the frosting – the bottom side of the top cake should be facing up. Place the cake on a cake plate or cake board.

Coat the cake using the remaining frosting. Crumble the reserved trimmings with your fingertips to resemble fine breadcrumbs. Use to decorate the base and top edge of the cake. Chill for at least 30 minutes before serving. Decorate the top with the beetroot/beet crisps.

Top tip
You will not need all of these for the decoration, so sprinkle some fine rock salt over the remainder and enjoy as a snack.

Queen of Sheba cake

Less is more with the elegant single layer Queen of Sheba cake –
although I couldn't resist a few gold vegan sprinkles!

175 g/³⁄₄ cup plain/all-purpose
    flour
75 g/³⁄₄ cup ground almonds
2¹⁄₂ tablespoons unsweetened
    cocoa powder
140 g/scant ³⁄₄ cup caster/
    superfine sugar, plus
    1 tablespoon
2¹⁄₂ teaspoons baking powder
1¹⁄₄ teaspoons bicarbonate
    of soda/baking soda
240 g/scant 1¹⁄₄ cup soya/
    soy yogurt
90 ml/¹⁄₃ cup sunflower oil
1 tablespoon golden/light
    corn syrup
115 ml/¹⁄₂ cup chickpea/
    garbanzo bean water
¹⁄₂ teaspoon distilled white
    vinegar
¹⁄₂ teaspoon salt
¹⁄₄ quantity of Vegan Chocolate
    Fudge Icing (see page 23),
    made with 30 g/1 oz. vegan
    butter, 80 g/generous ¹⁄₃ cup
    soya/soy yogurt, ¹⁄₂ teaspoon
    pure vanilla extract, 35 g/
    ¹⁄₃ cup unsweetened cocoa
    powder and 45 g/
    5 tablespoons icing/
    confectioners' sugar
50 g/generous ¹⁄₂ cup flaked/
    sliced almonds
1¹⁄₂ tablespoons vegan gold
    sprinkles (I like Gold
    Confetti Sequins from
    Bakingtimeclub.com,
    see suppliers, page 142)

*20-cm/8-inch cake pan,
greased and lined*

Serves 10–12

Preheat the oven to 180°C (350°F) Gas 4.

Sift the flour into a large bowl, add the ground almonds,
cocoa powder, caster/superfine sugar, baking powder and
bicarbonate of soda/baking soda, and mix with a spoon
to combine. Make a well in the middle.

Put the soya/soy yogurt into a bowl and add the sunflower
oil and golden/light corn syrup. Mix with a spoon until
fully combined. Pour into the well of dry ingredients.
Fold through with a spatula or wooden spoon until just
combined and smooth.

With a hand-held electric whisk, whisk the chickpea/
garbanzo bean water, vinegar and salt until soft peaks
form. Add the tablespoon of caster/superfine sugar
and whisk until stiff peaks form. Fold a quarter through
the cake mix, then, when mostly combined, fold the
next quarter through, and continue until the whisked
chickpea/garbanzo bean water is used up.

Transfer to the greased and lined pan. Bake in the
preheated oven for 35–40 minutes; you are looking for
firm edges and an ever so slightly soft centre to give it
that traditional creaminess. Allow the cake to cool in the
pan for 10 minutes, then carefully remove and transfer
to a wire rack to cool completely. It may have a slight
dip, but this is quite usual for this type of cake. Once cool
level the surface with a sharp serrated knife and invert.

Place the cake onto a cake plate or serving platter and
coat in the chocolate fudge icing. Press the almond flakes
onto the sides, then press on the gold sprinkles.

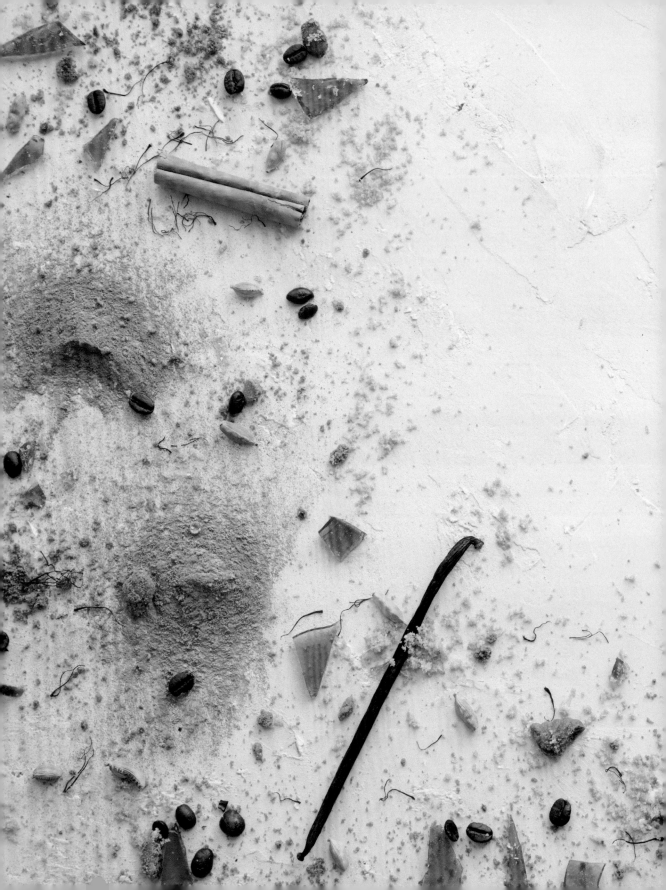

Sugar & Spice

Salted caramel drip cake

The delicious caramel sauce on top of this show-stopper oozes style and flavour.

1 quantity of Vegan Deep Vanilla Sponge mixture (see page 15), swapping the caster/superfine sugar for light soft brown sugar for a caramel flavour, and adding 1–2 teaspoons rock salt, baked in 3 greased and lined 18-cm/7-inch cake pans for 30 minutes until an inserted cocktail stick/toothpick comes out clean, then cooled

1 quantity of Simple Vegan Vanilla Buttercream (see page 20)

1 quantity of Soft Vegan Caramel Sauce (see page 24), with 1 teaspoon sea salt stirred through with the melted coconut oil

HAZELNUT TOPPERS
20–25 hazelnuts (you may not need all of these, but it's good to have a few spare)
200 g/1 cup caster/superfine sugar
20–25 cocktail sticks/toothpicks

Serves 20

Trim the tops of the cakes to make level if necessary. Sandwich together using 350 g/12 oz. of the vegan vanilla buttercream – the bottom side of the top cake should be facing up. Place the cake on a cake plate or cake board.

Use 450 g/1 lb. of the buttercream to crumb coat the cake (see page 12). Place in the fridge for 15 minutes, then use the remaining buttercream to coat the cake in a second layer.

Push a cocktail stick/toothpick into each hazelnut, away from the seam. Place a large sheet of baking parchment on the floor just below where you are working, and have a heavy chopping board at the ready.

Place a medium saucepan over a medium heat. Add the sugar and heat until dissolved. Swirl the pan from time to time until the sugar is fully dissolved and the caramel is a deep amber colour. Remove from the heat.

Allow the caramel to cool and thicken a little. One at a time, dredge a hazelnut through the thickened caramel, coating it very generously. Secure the cocktail stick/toothpick on the work surface under the chopping board, so the caramel-covered hazelnut hangs over the edge of the work surface. Allow the caramel to drip like a stalactite towards the parchment-covered floor and set hard.

Arrange a few spikes on the side of the cake. You can leave the side spikes on the cocktail sticks/toothpicks to help angle them. Put 2 teaspoons of the soft caramel sauce in the middle of the top of the cake. Spread out a little and arrange the hazelnut spikes on top. Pour the remaining soft caramel sauce around it and spread out with a dinner or palette knife until it meets the caramel sauce where the spikes are sitting and starts to drip down the sides of the cake.

Honeycomb cake

It's great finding confectionery that's much simpler than I ever imagined to make – and using only 3 vegan-friendly ingredients!

1 quantity of Vegan Deep Vanilla Sponge mixture (see page 15), swapping the caster/superfine sugar for soft light brown sugar, baked in 3 greased and lined 18-cm/7-inch cake pans for 30–35 minutes until an inserted cocktail stick/toothpick comes out clean, then cooled

1 quantity of Simple Vegan Vanilla Buttercream (see page 20)

HONEYCOMB/SPONGE CANDY
2 teaspoons bicarbonate of soda/baking soda
200 g/1 cup caster/superfine sugar
5 tablespoons golden/light corn syrup
20-cm/8-inch square pan, greased

Serves 20

For the honeycomb/sponge candy, put the bicarbonate of soda/baking soda into a little bowl. In a deep saucepan, stir the caster/superfine sugar and golden/light corn syrup together over a gentle heat until melted. Try not to let the mixture bubble too much – stirring will help.

Once melted, turn up the heat a little until amber in colour, then quickly remove from the heat, pour in the bicarbonate of soda/baking soda in one go, and beat with a wooden spoon until it has disappeared and the mixture is foaming. Transfer to the greased pan immediately.

The mixture will continue to bubble. Simply leave it in the pan for about 1 hour 30 minutes until hard. Once hard, snap into large chunks. Set aside.

Trim the tops of the cakes to make level if necessary. Sandwich together using 350 g/12 oz. of the buttercream – the bottom side of the top cake should be facing up. Place the cake on a cake plate or cake board.

Use 450 g/1 lb. of the buttercream to crumb coat the cake (see page 12). Place in the fridge for 30 minutes.

Blitz 35 g/1¼ oz. of the honeycomb/sponge candy in a food processor to fine crumbs. Loosely fold most of the crumbs through the remaining buttercream and use to coat the cake in a second layer (this time use sweeping motions – this not only gives a nice texture, but helps make things a little easier if you have the odd larger crumb). Position the large pieces of honeycomb/sponge candy on top of the cake. Dust the sides and top with the remaining honeycomb/sponge candy crumbs.

Store honeycomb/sponge candy in a sealed container in a cool, dry place. Decorate on the day of serving. If there are leftovers, remove from the cake and store in a sealed container or zip-lock bag. Serve alongside the cake.

Tipsy tiramisu cake

Tiramisu. The perfect way to end a meal, literally translating as 'pick me up'. I love the idea of making this decadent dessert in cake-form, making it easy to have a 'pick me up!' any time of day.

1 quantity of Vegan Deep Vanilla Sponge mixture (see page 15), adding 4 heaped teaspoons instant espresso coffee powder to the dry mix, baked in 3 greased and lined 18-cm/7-inch cake pans for 30 minutes until an inserted cocktail stick/toothpick comes out clean, then cooled

4–6 tablespoons Masala, for brushing

unsweetened cocoa powder, for dusting

FROSTING
400 g/14 oz. vegan butter
800 g/5¾ cups icing/ confectioners' sugar
150 g/5 oz. vegan cream cheese

disposable piping/pastry bag fitted with a 1-cm/³⁄₈-inch round nozzle/tip

Serves 20

For the frosting, place the vegan butter, icing/ confectioners' sugar and vegan cream cheese in a food processor and pulse until blended. Set aside 300 g/10½ oz. of the frosting; cover and chill.

Trim the tops of the cakes to make level if necessary. Halve the cakes horizontally. Sandwich together using 375 g/13 oz. of the frosting, brushing each sponge with a little Masala as you go – the bottom side of the top cake should be facing up. Place the cake on a cake plate or cake board.

Coat the cake using the remaining frosting. Chill for 30 minutes. Put the reserved frosting in the piping/ pastry bag and cover the top of the cake with little swirls. Chill for 30 minutes.

Dust the top with plenty of cocoa powder.

Coffee & cardamom curious cake

Here the fragrant touch of cardamom gives a soft edge to punchy, zingy coffee cake.

6 green cardamom pods
2 black cardamom pods
  (optional, see top tip)
315 g/scant 2½ cups
  plain/all-purpose flour
185 g/scant 1 cup caster/
  superfine sugar
3½ teaspoons baking powder
1¼ teaspoons bicarbonate
  of soda/baking soda
320 g/1½ cups soya/
  soy yogurt
120 ml/½ cup sunflower oil
1½ tablespoons golden/
  light corn syrup
1 teaspoon vanilla extract
6 tablespoons strong black
  coffee, cooled
75 g/⅔ cup pecan nuts,
  roughly chopped

FILLING & DECORATION
½ quantity of Simple Vegan
  Vanilla Buttercream (see
  page 20), but replace the
  water with 1 tablespoon
  instant coffee granules
  mixed with 2 tablespoons
  just-boiled water
1 tablespoon cocoa power
20–24 coffee beans
*2 x 20-cm/8-inch cake pans,
  greased and lined*
*disposable piping/pastry bag
  fitted with a large star
  nozzle/tip*

Serves 12

Preheat the oven to 180°C (350°F) Gas 4.

Crush the cardamom pods to open the shells, then coarsely grind the seeds with a pestle and mortar, and place into a large bowl.

Sift the flour into the bowl, add the sugar, baking powder and bicarbonate of soda/baking soda, and mix with a spoon to combine. Make a well in the middle.

Put the soya/soy yogurt into a bowl, add the sunflower oil, golden/light corn syrup, vanilla extract and strong black coffee. Mix with a spoon until fully combined. Pour into the well of dry ingredients. Fold through with a spatula or wooden spoon until combined and smooth. Fold through the pecan nuts.

Spoon into the cake pans and bake for 30–35 minutes until an inserted cocktail stick/toothpick comes out clean. Leave to cool in the pans for 10 minutes, then transfer to wire racks to cool completely.

Place one of the cakes on a cake plate or cake board. Fill the piping/pastry bag with 450 g/1 lb. of the coffee buttercream and pipe a closed 'S' shape all around the edge. Continue this pattern inwards, this will be inside the cake so you don't need to be too neat here.

With the second cake on the work surface, use 85 g/3 oz. of the remaining buttercream to spread a thin layer over the top – leaving a 1.5-cm/½-inch border all around the edge. Sift over the cocoa powder so it sticks to the buttercream.

Fill the piping/pastry bag with the remaining buttercream and pipe the closed 'S' shape, so the buttercream covers the border and edge of the cocoa powder. Place on top of the base cake. Decorate with coffee beans.

Top tip
Black cardamom gives a slightly smoky flavour – simply switch for two extra green cardamom pods if you prefer.

Chai-spiced cupcakes

Let a chai-spiced tea-bag do the hard work! By adding the contents directly to the batter mix, not a smidge of flavour is lost.

1 chai-spiced tea bag
½ quantity of Vegan Deep Vanilla Sponge mixture (see page 15)
½ quantity of Vegan Biscuit/Cookie Thins dough (see page 27)
plain/all-purpose flour, for dusting
½ quantity of Simple Vegan Vanilla Buttercream (see page 20)
1 cinnamon stick, broken into 10–12 long shards
5-cm/2-inch piece of fresh ginger, finely sliced with a vegetable peeler or mandoline into 10–12 slices
nutmeg, for grating
12-hole muffin pan, lined with paper cases
1 diamond or fan-shaped cutter
baking sheet, lined
disposable piping/pastry bag fitted with a 1.5-cm/½-inch plain round nozzle/tip

Makes 10–12

Preheat the oven to 180°C (350°F) Gas 4.

Cut open the tea bag and stir the contents into the sponge mixture, then divide the mixture between the paper cases (it will make 10–12 depending on the size of your cases) and bake in the preheated oven for 25 minutes, until an inserted cocktail stick/toothpick comes out clean. Allow to cool in the pan for 10 minutes, then remove and place on a wire rack to cool completely.

Meanwhile prepare the vegan biscuit/cookie thins. Roll a walnut-sized piece of dough in your hands, then roll it out between two pieces of baking parchment, dusting a little flour on the base parchment and on top of the dough if necessary. Stamp out a diamond or fan shape using a cutter, and transfer to the lined baking sheet. Repeat until you have one for each of your cupcakes.

Fill a piping/pastry bag with the buttercream and pipe a swirl on the top of each cake. Decorate each cake with a shaped vegan biscuit/cookie thin, a shard of cinnamon, a piece of ginger and a grating of nutmeg.

Lotus Biscoff traybake

There's only one way to celebrate this vegan gem – put it into cake!

10 Lotus Biscoff
biscuits/cookies
1 quantity of Vegan Terrific
Traybake Sponge mixture
(page 19)

FROSTING
300 g/generous 2 cups
icing/confectioners' sugar
100 g/3½ oz. vegan butter,
softened
100 g/3½ oz. Lotus Biscoff
spread

DECORATION
6 Lotus Biscoff biscuits/cookies
1 quantity of Soft Vegan
Caramel Sauce
(see page 24), made with
2 tablespoons almond
butter, 1 tablespoon golden/
light corn syrup and
1½ teaspoons coconut oil
(add another ½–1 teaspoon
melted coconut oil, to get a
good drizzling consistency,
if necessary)
20 x 30-cm/8 x 12-inch cake
pan, greased and lined

Serves 15

Pulse the biscuits/cookies in a food processor so they are mostly fine crumbs but with a few bigger lumps for a bit of texture (or place in a sealable/zip-lock bag and bash with a rolling pin). Stir the crumbs through the sponge batter.

Spoon into the cake pan and bake in the preheated oven for 35–40 minutes until an inserted cocktail stick/toothpick comes out clean. Allow to cool in the pan for 10 minutes, then carefully invert onto a chopping board to remove from the pan, then invert again onto a cooling rack to cool completely.

Place all the frosting ingredients in a bowl. Whisk with a hand-held electric whisk, adding 1–2 teaspoons of just-boiled water to loosen, if necessary.

Use a dinner knife to coat the top of the traybake in the frosting. Decorate with a fan of 3 biscuits/cookies. Put the remaining biscuits/cookies in a bag and bash with a rolling pin to crush roughly. Scatter over the top of the cake. Finish with a drizzle of soft caramel sauce.

S'mores dip cake

Who needs a campfire for this campfire treat?! There's not much that can beat melted marshmallows sandwiched between two biscuits, but take these yummy components and serve on a creamy-chocolately-biscuity surprise-inside cake and dive in!

1 quantity of Vegan Biscuit/
Cookie Thins dough
(see page 27)
1 quantity of Vegan Deep
Vanilla Sponge mixture
(see page 15)
2 tablespoons good-quality
cocoa powder mixed with
4 tablespoons just-boiled
water

FILLING & TOPPING
400 g/14 oz. Lotus Biscoff
Spread
5 tablespoons unsweetened
cocoa powder
250 ml/1 cup plant cream
200 g/7 oz. vegan
marshmallows

TO SERVE
4 figs, cut into wedges
4 plums, stoned/pitted and
cut into wedges
baking sheet, lined
2 x 20-cm/8-inch cake pans,
greased and lined

Serves 12

Preheat the oven to 180°C (350°F) Gas 4.

For the biscuits/cookies, roll out the dough between two pieces of baking parchment. Cut 12 rectangular biscuits/cookies 7.5 x 5 cm/3 x 2 inches. Transfer to the lined baking sheet and use a fork to make 'dots' in each biscuit/cookie. Chill for 15 minutes, then bake for 20 minutes until light golden brown. Transfer to a cooling rack to cool.

Divide the cake mix between two bowls. Fold the cocoa powder mix through one bowl. Leave the second bowl plain.

Spoon the vanilla mix into one cake pan and the chocolate mix into the other. Bake for 30–35 minutes until an inserted cocktail stick/toothpick comes out clean. Leave to cool in the pans for 10 minutes, then transfer to wire racks to cool completely.

Trim the tops of the cakes to make level. Using a small upturned bowl or saucer as a guide, cut out a circle, 12.5-cm/5-inch in diameter, in the vanilla cake. Discard or use for another recipe – perfect for the cakesicle recipe on page 127.

Stir the Lotus Biscoff Spread to loosen it, then take 375 g/13 oz. of the spread and mix with the cocoa powder until it is a glossy chocolate frosting. Cover and set aside 160 g/5$\frac{1}{2}$ oz. of the chocolate frosting.

Place the chocolate cake on a cake plate or cake board. Spread 100 g/3$\frac{1}{2}$ oz. of the Biscoff chocolate frosting over the top to cover. Place the vanilla sponge ring on top. Use the remaining frosting to coat the outside of the cake in a thin layer. Set aside.

Whip the plant cream until very soft peaks form. Stir the cream through the reserved Biscoff chocolate frosting, a couple of tablespoons at a time.

Fill the middle recess with the Biscoff chocolate cream filling (reserving 3 tablespoons). Cover with the marshmallows. Using a dinner knife, palette knife or metal spatula, smear the reserved 3 tablespoons of cream filling and the remaining 25 g/1 oz. of Biscoff spread around the sides of the cake to decorate.

Serve with the biscuits/cookies, fruit and skewers.

Vanilla mini Bundts with vanilla & saffron soya custard

These cute little Bundts are delicious cooled or make a decadent dessert; serve warm with this steamy soy milk vanilla and saffron custard.

½ quantity of Vegan Deep Vanilla Sponge mixture (see page 15), adding the seeds from 1 vanilla pod/bean to the 'wet' mix. Divide between 8 greased 100-ml/3¾-fl oz. mini Bundt moulds. Bake for 20–25 minutes until an inserted cocktail stick/toothpick comes out clean, then cool until just warm

SOYA/SOY CUSTARD
3½ tablespoons cornflour/cornstarch
500 ml/2 cups soya/soy milk, plus 1 tablespoon
1 tablespoon caster/superfine sugar
½ teaspoon saffron strands, plus extra to decorate
seeds from 1 vanilla pod/bean
pinch turmeric (optional)

Makes 8

Trim the flat 'top' of each Bundt to make level; this will become the base.

For the custard, put the cornflour/cornstarch in a small bowl and stir through 60 ml/¼ cup of the soya/soy milk to create a paste.

Put the remaining 440 ml/1¾ cups soya milk in a saucepan with the sugar, saffron strands and vanilla seeds. Place over a medium heat and heat, stirring, until lukewarm, whisk in the cornflour/cornstarch paste.

Continue to whisk and bring the custard up to a simmer, and continuously whisk until thickened. Cook for a further minute (add the turmeric at this stage if you prefer a slightly more yellow colour). Allow to cool a little while continuing to whisk. If you prefer it a little thinner, gradually dribble in the 1 tablespoon soya/soy milk while continuing to whisk.

Decorate the Bundts with the extra saffron strands. Pour the custard over the Bundts to serve.

Top tip

This is plenty of custard to serve 4. You may like 2 Bundts each, or you can freeze the extras for up to 3 months. Wrap individually in clingfilm/plastic wrap. Allow to defrost, then warm in the microwave for 10–20 seconds.

Sticky date & polenta traybake

Texture from the polenta and a gorgeous toffee flavour from brown sugar and sticky dates make this blondie-style traybake completely moreish.

325 g/11½ oz. dates,
   roughly chopped
275 g/scant 1¼ cups soya/soy
   yogurt, plus 3 tablespoons
175 g/¾ cup plain/all-purpose
   flour
50 g/⅓ cup polenta/cornmeal
150 g/¾ cup caster/superfine
   sugar
250 g/1¼ cup light soft
   brown sugar
1 teaspoon baking powder
250 g/9 oz. vegan butter,
   melted
1 teaspoon pure vanilla
   extract
1 quantity of Soft Vegan
   Caramel Sauce
   (see page 24, optional)
*20 x 30-cm/8 x 12-inch cake
   pan, greased and lined*

Makes 15

Preheat the oven to 180°C (350°F) Gas 4.

Put 100 g/3½ oz. of the dates with the 3 tablespoons of soya/soy yogurt in a mini food processor and blend to a coarse purée. Set aside.

Put the flour in a large bowl with the polenta/cornmeal, caster/superfine sugar, light brown sugar and baking powder. Mix well to combine. Create a well in the middle.

Add the melted vegan butter, vanilla extract and soya/soy yogurt to the well, fold with a wooden spoon or spatula to combine to make a thick batter. Fold through the coarsely puréed dates, then most of the chopped dates.

Spoon into the prepared pan and level the surface. Scatter over the remaining dates. Bake for 35–45 minutes until an inserted cocktail stick/toothpick comes out clean around the edges – you still want it to be a little sticky in the middle. Allow to cool completely in the pan on a wire rack. Turn out and cut into 15 squares.

Pile the squares onto a cake stand and drizzle with the soft caramel sauce, if you like.

Lemon & ginger teacake

Steeping the fruit in a mix of English breakfast and lemon and ginger tea, gives the fruits in this cake a fragrant plump texture and the cake a delicious, moist quality.

2 lemon and ginger teabags
1 English breakfast teabag
350 ml/1½ cups just boiled water
175 g/1¼ cups dried mixed fruit
100 g/½ cup caster/superfine sugar
½ quantity of Vegan Deep Vanilla Sponge mixture (see page 15)

TO DECORATE
200 g/1 cup caster/superfine sugar
3 lemons, 2 sliced and 1 pared
½ quantity of Vegan Royal Icing (see page 24)

BRANDY SNAPS (OPTIONAL, SEE TOP TIP)
50 g/2 oz. vegan butter
50 g/¼ cup brown sugar
50 g/2½ tablespoons golden/light corn syrup
50 g/6 tablespoons plain/all-purpose flour
½ teaspoon ground ginger
grated zest of ½ lemon, plus 1 teaspoon freshly squeezed juice
1 teaspoon brandy
20-cm/8-inch Bundt pan, greased
2 baking sheets, lined

Serves 10–12

Preheat the oven to 180°C (350°F) Gas 4.

Put the tea bags into a measuring jug/cup and pour over the just-boiled water. Allow to steep for 10 minutes.

Put the dried fruit into a saucepan with the sugar. Remove the teabags from the tea, and pour the tea over the fruit. Bring to the boil and simmer, stirring, for 4 minutes. Allow to cool. Drain; discard the liquid.

Fold the fruit through the cake mixture. Transfer to the greased Bundt pan and bake in the preheated oven for 45 minutes. Allow to cool in the pan for 10 minutes, then invert onto a wire rack to cool completely.

Meanwhile make the candied lemon slices and curls for the decoration. In a saucepan, combine the sugar with 250 ml/1 cup of water and bring to the boil over a medium-high heat, stirring until the sugar dissolves. Add the lemon slices and pared lemon strips. Simmer for 5–6 minutes until the pith and lemon become semi translucent. Using a slotted spoon, transfer to a wire rack set over a baking sheet to cool. Discard the syrup. When the strips are cool enough to handle bend into interesting shapes or wind around wooden spoon handles.

For the brandy snaps, preheat the oven to 180°C (350°F) Gas 4. Put the vegan butter, sugar and syrup in a saucepan and heat gently until the butter and sugar have melted. Put the flour and ginger in a bowl and make a well in the centre. Add the lemon zest and juice, and brandy. Pour in the vegan butter mixture and gradually beat it in until smooth.

Use a teaspoon to dollop 8 mounds of the mixture across the two baking sheets, well spaced apart. Cook for 8–10 minutes until golden (cook any extra mixture in batches afterwards). Leave for a minute or two before shaping. They should be pliable, but set enough to bend without tearing. Wrap around wood spoon handles for a cigar shape.

Drizzle the cake with the vegan royal icing and decorate with the bandy snaps, lemon shapes and slices.

Top tip
This makes around 12 brandy snaps – you will not need all of these to decorate the cake, but they can be kept for up to a week in a sealed airtight container – why not pipe whipped vegan cream inside each one for another decadent afternoon tea treat!

Party Time

Veganuary va va voom cake!

1 quantity of Vegan Chocolate Sponge mixture (see page 16), baked in 3 greased and lined 18-cm/7-inch cake pans for 30 minutes until an inserted cocktail stick/toothpick comes out clean, then cooled

½ quantity of Simple Vegan Vanilla Buttercream (see page 20)

CANDIED ORANGE
200 g/1 cup caster/superfine sugar
1 orange, cut into 3 mm/⅛ inch thick slices, seeds removed (cut a couple of slices in half, keep the remainder whole)

MERINGUE KISSES
vegan orange paste colouring
1 quantity of Vegan Meringue (see page 27, make this just before piping)

CROCCANTE
200 g/1 cup caster/superfine sugar
100 g/1¼ cups flaked almonds, toasted

FRESH FRUIT & HERBS
A few cranberries or red currants
3 physallis
2 sprigs of rosemary
50 g/2 oz. apple crisp (see top tip)
3 baking sheets, lined
1 piping/pastry bag
1 baking sheet, oiled

Serves 20

Preheat the oven to 100°C (200°F) Gas ¼.

For the dehydrated candied orange, in a saucepan combine the sugar with 200 ml/scant 1 cup of water. Bring to the boil over a medium-high heat, stirring until the sugar dissolves. Add the orange slices and simmer for 5–6 minutes. Use a slotted spoon to remove. When cool enough to handle, place onto one of the lined baking sheets.

Bake in the preheated oven for 2–4 hours, rotating every 2 hours. Allow to cool – they will crisp as they cool. Store any leftovers in an airtight container at room temperature for up to 1 month.

For the meringue kisses, prepare the piping/pastry bag before making the meringue. Turn the piping bag inside-out over a bottle. Paint stripes in the orange colouring down the sides of the bag. Make the meringue mixture and fill the bag with the meringue, ensuring there's enough room to twist the top. Snip a 1.5-cm/½-inch hole at the tip and pipe small blobs onto two of the lined baking sheets. Bake for 1 hour 15 minutes–1 hour 30 minutes until the undersides are dry and can be lifted easily from the baking parchment. (This will make around 25 meringue kisses – you will not need all of these, but leftovers are lovely simply served with a coffee or crushed into whipped vegan cream with chopped strawberries for that classic British dessert, Eton Mess.)

For the croccante, put the sugar in a saucepan. Cook over a medium heat, without stirring (swirl the pan a little, if necessary), until the sugar melts and turns a golden colour. Add the almonds and carry on cooking for 30 seconds–1 minute. Pour onto the oiled baking sheet and leave to cool and set. Roughly break up the croccante into shards. Set aside.

If necessary, trim the tops of the cakes so they are level. Sandwich the cakes together using 300 g/10½ oz. of the buttercream. The bottom side of the top cake should be facing up. Place the cake on a cake plate or cake board. Crumb coat (see page 12) the cake using the remaining buttercream. This will be your final coating giving it a semi-naked look; scrape off enough buttercream to reveal some of the sponge.

Decorate with the croccante, candied orange, meringue kisses, cranberries or red currants, physallis, rosemary sprigs and apple crisp.

Top tip
You can find ready-made versions of apple crisp fairly easily. For homemade, cut two eating apples across the core into 1–2-mm/¹⁄₁₆-inch slices. Lay on a baking sheet lined with baking parchment. Cook for 1½–2 hours at 80°C (160°F) until dried out (turn over after 1 hour).

Gin & tonic traybake

How to get the party started! The actual G&Ts might start
flowing while you're eating this one.

**finely grated zest and juice
of 2 limes, plus lime wedges
and pared zest to decorate**
**1 quantity of Vegan Terrific
Traybake Sponge mixture
(page 19)**
**60 g/generous ¼ cup
caster/superfine sugar,
plus extra for sprinkling**
60 ml/¼ cup gin
60 ml/¼ cup tonic
**120 g/4 oz. Simple Vegan
Vanilla Buttercream
(see page 20, optional) made
with 40 g/1½ oz. vegan
butter and 80 g/½ cup icing/
confectioners' sugar**
mint leaves, to decorate
straws, to decorate (optional)
*20 x 30-cm/8 x 12-inch cake
pan, greased and lined*

Serves 15

Preheat the oven to 180°C (350°F) Gas 4.

Stir the finely grated lime zest through the cake batter.
Spoon into the cake pan. Bake in the preheated oven
for 40 minutes until an inserted cocktail stick/ toothpick
comes out clean. Allow to cool in the pan for 10 minutes.

Meanwhile, put the sugar into a pan with the lime juice,
gin and tonic. Place the pan on a medium heat and allow
to bubble until the sugar has dissolved and the liquid has
reduced slightly.

Prick the top of the cake with a fork and spoon over half
the syrup. Allow to soak in, then spoon over the remainder
to taste. Once fully soaked and almost cool, invert onto
a chopping board, then invert again onto a cooling rack
to cool completely.

Sprinkle over some caster/superfine sugar and decorate
with small spoonfuls of buttercream, if liked. Insert a
straw into each buttercream mound, if using, and add
the extra lime zest and mint leaves.

Oil-painted buttercream cake

Fancy yourself as Vincent Van Gogh? Let it out in vegan buttercream!

1 quantity of Simple Vegan
  Vanilla Buttercream
  (see page 20)
vegan pink colouring
  (optional, see page 11)
1 quantity of Vegan Deep
  Vanilla Sponge mixture
  (see page 15) baked in
  3 greased and lined
  18-cm/7-inch cake pans
  for 30 minutes until
  an inserted cocktail stick/
  toothpick comes out
  clean, then cooled
50 g/2 oz. dark/bittersweet
  vegan chocolate, melted

FLOWER TOPPERS
vegan pink colouring
  (see page 11)
175 g/6 oz. vegan white
  flower sugarpaste
25 g/1 oz. vegan gold
  sugar pearls
5-cm/2-inch flower cutter
3-cm/1¼-inch flower cutter
6–8 clean spice lids
1 medium paint brush

Serves 20

Put 175 g/6 oz. of the buttercream into a bowl. For the petal buttercream 'paint', mix in enough colouring to get a light shade of pink. Remove 30 g/1 oz. of the buttercream and reserve. Add a little more colouring to get a mid-tone. Remove 30 g/1 oz. of the buttercream. Add a little more colouring to get a slightly darker tone for the remaining buttercream. This gives three tones to work from as you wish.

For the flower toppers, knead enough colouring into the white flower sugarpaste to get a light–mid shade of pink. Roll out as thinly as possible on baking parchment. Stamp out 6 larger flower shapes and 6–8 smaller flower shapes. Brush the inner part of the larger flowers with the darker shade of buttercream; leave these larger flowers to dry out overnight in clean up-turned spice lids to shape. Pinch the bases of the smaller flowers to ruche. Set aside on parchment to dry out. Cover the bowls of coloured buttercream with clingfilm/plastic wrap until needed again.

Trim the tops of the cakes to make level if necessary. Sandwich the cakes together using 350 g/12 oz. of the plain buttercream – the bottom side of the top cake should be facing up. Place the cake on a cake plate or board.

Use 450 g/1 lb. of the plain buttercream to crumb coat the cake (see page 12). Place in the fridge for 15 minutes, then use the remaining plain buttercream to coat the cake in a second layer. Chill for at least 1 hour.

When ready to decorate, brush the branches on free-hand using the melted chocolate. Return to the fridge for 15 minutes to set.

Give each of the pink buttercream shades a stir to loosen, adding a drop of water if necessary. Using a mini palette knife or metal spatula, pick up a small amount of the pink buttercream (using the shade(s) of your choice) on the very tip and smear on the cake to make a petal shape. Repeat to make a flower shape. You may wish to add highlights and shadows with the other shades of buttercream, using the brush. Repeat until you have covered your branches, as liked. Chill the cake every now and then to keep the base (your canvas!) firm, if necessary.

Brush some of the small sugarpaste flowers with the buttercream to create highlights and shadows, if liked. Gently press onto the side of the cake and position the remaining larger flowers on the top of the cake. Drop several gold sugar pearls into the middle of the larger sugarpaste flowers on the top of the cake and use to decorate the middle of the smaller buttercream flowers.

Neapolitan cakes in jars

A gorgeous little edible gift, with a recipe that makes two...
well you've got to treat yourself, too!

½ quantity of **Vegan Deep Vanilla Sponge** mixture (see page 15)

vegan strong pink paste or gel food colouring

⅛ teaspoon **vegan strawberry flavouring**

1 teaspoon **unsweetened cocoa powder** mixed with 1 teaspoon **just-boiled water**, plus extra for dusting

Simple Vegan Vanilla Buttercream (see page 20) made with 100 g/3½ oz. butter, a few drops of vanilla extract and 200 g/scant 1½ cups icing/confectioners' sugar (omit the water)

1 **strawberry**, halved, to decorate

20 x 30-cm/8 x 12-inch baking tray with sides, greased

5–7-cm/2–3-inch round cutter (depending on your jars)

disposable piping/pastry bag fitted with a medium star nozzle/tip

2 clean, dry jam jars

Makes 2

Preheat the oven to 180°C (350°F) Gas 4.

Position the greased baking tray with one of the long sides facing you. Cut some baking parchment into a long strip 20 cm/8 inches wide, so it fits the base exactly, but allow the right and left side of the parchment to hang over the right and left side each by about 20 cm/8 inches. Pinch the parchment one-third of the way along and then pinch again so you are left with 3 equal sized spaces – you are aiming to divide the tray into thirds. Use the overhanging parchment to line the sides of the tray, then trim.

Divide the cake batter between three bowls. Stir the vegan pink colouring and flavouring through one portion, stir the cocoa mix through the second portion and leave the third portion plain. Spoon the three mixes into the spaces in the baking tray. Bake in the preheated oven for 30 minutes until an inserted cocktail stick/toothpick comes out clean.

Allow to cool in the tray for 10 minutes, then invert and allow to cool completely on a cooling rack. Using the round cutter, stamp out two rounds from each flavour (reserve the trimmings for recipes such as Super-Stylish Cakesicles on page 127).

Fill the disposable piping/pastry bag with the buttercream and pipe a layer in the bottom of both jars. Add alternate layers of cake and buttercream to the jars, finishing with buttercream on top. Decorate each with a dusting of cocoa powder and a fresh strawberry half.

Gifting tip

These make lovely gifts! Tie a ribbon around the neck of the jar, add a gift tag and even attach a little wooden tea spoon. If giving as gifts you may want to take the strawberries separately with you! Or scatter with vegan sprinkles or freeze-dried fruit pieces.

Super-stylish cakesicles

There's no need for warm weather to enjoy cakesicles! From birthday parties
to fun wedding favours, these elegant lollies taste as good as they look.

320 g/11 oz. vegan white
  chocolate, melted
225 g/8 oz. vegan cake
  trimmings or leftover vegan
  chocolate or vanilla sponge
90 g/3 oz. Simple Vegan
  Vanilla Buttercream
  (see page 20), made
  with 60 g/½ cup icing/
  confectioners' sugar,
  a few drops of pure vanilla
  extract and 30 g/1 oz. vegan
  butter (omit the water)
pink vegan food colouring
  (optional, see colour tip)
1 teaspoon dried rose petals
white vegan edible pearls,
  to decorate
pink vegan edible pearls,
  to decorate
4 x 100-ml/3½-fl oz. cakesicle
  moulds
4 wooden lollipop/popsicle sticks

Makes 4

Melt 100 g/3½ oz. of the chocolate in the microwave in 30-second bursts
or in a bain marie. Brush the inside of the cakesicle cavities with the
melted chocolate. Insert and remove a lollipop/popsicle stick to leave a
hole in the wet chocolate. Chill in the fridge for 30 minutes (or freeze for
15 minutes). Repeat the process with another 100 g/3½ oz. of chocolate.

While the second coat is setting in the fridge or freezer, crumble the cake
and mix the cake with enough of the buttercream until the mixture just
holds together.

Once the chocolate has set, carefully press the cake into the chocolate
shells. Leave a 1-mm/1⁄16-inch gap at the top. Insert a lollipop/popsicle
stick into each of the holes (see top tip), then level the top surface with
your finger tips.

Melt 80 g/3 oz. of the remaining chocolate, and use it to cover the
exposed cake on each cakesicle and smooth off using a palette knife
or metal spatula. Freeze for 2 hours; this will help them firm up,
making them easier to remove from the mould.

Carefully release from the mould. Chill until ready to decorate.

Melt the remaining chocolate and colour it pink with a little colouring,
if using. Drizzle over the cakesicles and sprinkle over the dried rose
petals and vegan pearls. To position individual edible pearls, simply
dot them with any chocolate left in the bowl and use like a glue to
stick them to the cakesicles.

Colour tip
There are now vegan paste and gel colourings available, but colourings
and chocolate aren't always the best of friends. I loved stirring through
a touch of freeze-dried pink pitaya powder here to get that gorgeous
blush-shade. It's readily available online and a wonderfully natural
way to achieve all shades of pink!

Top tip
Heat the tip of a sharp knife and insert this into the stick hole just before
pushing the stick in for the final time, this will melt any chocolate that
may have covered the hole and prevent the chocolate cracking when
you push the lollipop/popsicle stick in.

Metallic marvel cupcakes

Extremely versatile, serve at any party from a glitzy, glamourous celebration through to an epic superhero birthday party!

½ quantity of Vegan Biscuit/Cookie Thins dough (see page 27)

plain/all-purpose flour, for dusting

100 g/3½ oz. vegan silver sprinkles

½ quantity of Simple Vegan Vanilla Buttercream (see page 20)

black vegan food colouring

½ quantity of Vegan Deep Vanilla Sponge mixture (see page 15) baked in 10–12 cupcake cases in a muffin pan for 20–25 minutes until an inserted cocktail stick/toothpick comes out clean, then cooled

vegan silver lustre spray (optional)

1 small star, 1 small rocket and 1 small round cutter

baking sheet, lined

2 disposable piping/pastry bags with the tips cut at around 1 cm/⅜ inch

1 disposable piping/pastry bag fitted with a large star nozzle/tip

Makes 10–12

Roll walnut-sized pieces of the vegan biscuit/cookie thins dough in your hands, then roll out between two pieces of baking parchment, dusting a little flour on the base parchment and on top of the dough, if necessary. Use the cutters to stamp out different shapes, then transfer to the lined baking sheet. Repeat until you have 10–12 (depending on how many cupcakes you made). Allow to cool completely.

Put the sprinkles on a side plate. Spread a little buttercream on the flat side of each biscuit/cookie, ensuring it goes right to the edges and is in a fairly thick, even layer. Dip the frosted side in the sprinkles until completely covered.

Divide the remaining buttercream into two bowls. Use the black vegan colouring to colour one portion grey. Fill one of the piping/pastry bags with the tip cut with the grey buttercream, and fill the other one with the white buttercream. Place both of these piping/pastry bags inside the piping/pastry bag fitted with the star nozzle/tip, and pipe a swirl on the top of each cupcake. Decorate each cake with a biscuit/cookie and spray with the lustre spray, if using.

Lemon & white chocolate Mother's Day cake

Thanks, mum! With fresh flowers, meringue kisses, chunky pieces of white chocolate and refreshing lemon zest, this mother's day cake won't be forgotten in a hurry.

finely grated zest of 2 lemons
100 g/3½ oz. white vegan chocolate, chopped
1 quantity of Vegan Deep Vanilla Sponge mixture (see page 15)
1 quantity of Simple Vegan Vanilla Buttercream (see page 20), replacing the water with fresh lemon juice
50 g/2 oz. vegan lemon curd (store-bought or see page 31)
edible or food-safe flowers, to decorate

MERINGUE KISSES & ROSES
purple and yellow vegan paste food colouring
1 quantity of Vegan Meringue (see page 27)
2 x disposable piping/pastry bags, one fitted with a 2D closed star nozzle/tip
2 baking sheets, lined
3 x 18-cm/7-inch cake pans

Serves 20

Preheat the oven to 120°C (240°F) Gas ½.

Prepare the piping/pastry bags before making the meringue for the kisses and roses. Turn one piping/pastry bag inside-out over a bottle. Paint stripes of the purple colouring down the sides of the bag. Reverse so the stripes are on the inside, snip a 1-cm/⅜-inch hole in the bottom. Fill the bag with half of the meringue, ensuring there's enough room to twist the top. Pipe small blobs onto the lined baking sheets. Add the yellow food colouring to the remaining meringue. Fill the bag fitted with the 2D nozzle/tip with the yellow meringue and pipe small stars, and swirls to look like roses. Bake for 1 hour 15 minutes–1 hour 30 minutes until the undersides are dry and can be lifted easily from the parchment.

For the cake, stir the finely grated lemon zest and white vegan chocolate through the sponge mix. Spoon into the cake pans. Bake for 30 minutes until an inserted cocktail stick/toothpick comes out clean. Leave to cool in the pans for 10 minutes, then transfer to wire racks to cool completely.

Trim the tops of the cakes to make level, and reserve 50 g/2 oz. of the trimmings (if you do not have that amount of trimmings, slice a little more horizontally from one of the cakes, until you have the full 50 g/2 oz.). Crumble the trimmings until they resemble breadcrumbs, then mix with 50 g/2 oz. of the buttecream. Cover and set aside.

Sandwich the cakes together using 350 g/12 oz. of the buttercream and the lemon curd – the bottom side of the top cake should be facing up. Place the cake on a cake plate or cake board.

Crumb coat (see page 12) the cake using 400 g/14 oz. of the buttercream. Place in the fridge 15 minutes. Use most of the remaining buttercream to coat the cake in a second layer. Smooth and remove the excess buttercream with a palette knife/metal spatula.

Use the reserved trimmings mix as a 'clay' to create a little mound on one side of the top of the cake. Spread the remaining buttercream over the 'mound' and use to stick on the flowers and meringue shapes – working down and across the cake.

Easter cuddles nest cake

Show-off your love for Super Spring! The perfect time to indulge. This multi-coloured vegan vanilla buttercreamed triple layered chocolate cake (!) also holds a wonderful vegan mini dark chocolate egg surprise! Yeah baby!

1 quantity of Vegan Chocolate Sponge mixture (see page 16), baked in 3 greased and lined 18-cm/7-inch cake pans for 30 minutes until an inserted cocktail stick/toothpick comes out clean, then cooled

225 g/8 oz. vegan mini dark chocolate eggs with crunchy coating (I like Doisy & Dam Good Eggs, see suppliers, page 142)

1 quantity of Simple Vegan Vanilla Buttercream (see page 20)

150 g/5 oz. vegan chocolate drops with crunchy coating (I like Doisy & Dam Good Eggs, see suppliers, page 142)

pink, blue and yellow vegan food colouring (see page 11)

1 x 25-g/1-oz. vermicelli nest

30 g/1 oz. dark/bittersweet vegan chocolate, broken into pieces

2 tablespoons pastel-coloured vegan sprinkles (I like Dr Oetker Unicorn sprinkles and Pastel Rainbow Confetti from Bakingtimeclub.com, see suppliers, page 142)

disposable piping/pastry bags fitted with a large star nozzle/tip

Serves 20

Trim the tops of the cakes to make level, if necessary. Push a clean soup can into the centre of each cake, twist the can and lift to remove a circle of cake. Slice one of the removed pieces in half horizontally and reserve.

Reserve a small handful of the vegan mini dark chocolate eggs. Sandwich the cakes together using 250 g/9 oz. of the simple vegan buttercream – the bottom side of the top cake should be facing up. Place the cake on a cake plate or cake board. Fill the middle with the remaining vegan mini dark chocolate eggs and the chocolate drops, then place the small reserved sponge circle on top to enclose them.

Reserve 125 g/4 oz. buttercream, cover and set aside. Crumb coat (see page 12) the cake using 450 g/1 lb. of the buttercream. Place in the fridge for 15 minutes. Put 325 g/11½ oz. buttercream into a bowl and colour it a light blue shade. Put 225 g/8 oz. buttercream into a second bowl and colour it a baby pink shade. Put the remaining buttercream into a third bowl and colour it a light yellow shade.

Spread the yellow buttercream around the base, covering one-third of the sides of the cake, followed by a row of pink and a row of blue, also coating the top of the cake with the blue buttercream. Smooth and remove the excess buttercream with a palette knife/metal spatula. Chill for 30 minutes.

For the nest, gently pull apart the vermicelli nest to loosen and open it.

Line a small deep cereal bowl with clingfilm/plastic wrap. Melt the chocolate in a heatproof bowl set over a pan of simmering water or in the microwave in 10-second bursts, stirring in-between each burst.

Allow the chocolate to cool a little. Place the vermicelli nest in the bowl of chocolate and coat using a spoon and your fingertips. Transfer to the bowl lined with clingfilm/plastic wrap and ease up the sides of the bowl to enhance the nest shape. Chill for 20 minutes.

Put the reserved buttercream in the piping/pastry bag and pipe little rosettes around the top of the cake. Scatter 1 tablespoon cake sprinkles over the top. Place the nest in the middle of the cake and fill with the reserved vegan mini dark chocolate eggs.

Father's Day stout cake

For Father's day or St Patrick's day, this cake is certain to hit the spot!

150 g/5 oz. vegan butter
225 ml/scant 1 cup stout
 or Guinness
480 g/3²/₃ cups plain/
 all-purpose flour
5¹/₂ tablespoons good-quality
 unsweetened cocoa powder
280 g/scant 1¹/₂ cups
 caster/superfine sugar
5 teaspoons baking powder
1¹/₂ teaspoons bicarbonate
 of soda/baking soda
2 tablespoons golden/
 light corn syrup
480 g/2¹/₄ cups soya/
 soy yogurt
vegan black food colouring
900 g/2 lb. Simple Vegan
 Vanilla Buttercream
 (see page 20), made with
 300 g/10¹/₂ oz. butter and
 600 g/4¹/₄ cups icing/
 confectioners' sugar
450 g/1 lb. (approx.
 ¹/₂ quantity) Cashew Nut
 Vanilla Frosting (see page
 23 and top tip)
3 x 18-cm/7-inch cake pans,
 greased and lined

Serves 20

Preheat the oven to 180°C (350°F) Gas 4.

Heat the vegan butter in a pan with the stout, stirring occasionally, until the butter has melted. Set aside to cool until lukewarm.

Sift the flour into a large bowl, add the cocoa powder, caster/superfine sugar, baking powder and bicarbonate of soda/baking soda, and stir to combine. Make a well in the middle.

Mix the golden/light corn syrup with the soya/soy yogurt. Pour into the well of dry ingredients, along with the stout and butter mixture. Fold through with a spatula or wooden spoon until just combined and smooth. Fold through enough black food colouring to make it a very dark brown colour.

Transfer to the greased and lined pans. Bake for 30–35 minutes until an inserted cocktail stick/toothpick comes out clean. Allow to cool in the pans for 10 minutes, then remove and place on wire racks to cool completely.

Mix the buttercream and the cashew nut frosting together in a bowl using a hand-held electric whisk set at slow speed until just combined. If it becomes a little loose, chill for 30–45 minutes – you want it to just hold its shape when spread with a knife.

Trim the cakes a little, but leave a slight peak to enhance the thick 'striped finish' of this cake. Sandwich the cakes together using 800 g/1 lb. 12 oz. of the cashew buttercream mix – the bottom side of the top cake should be facing up. Top generously with the remainder, create a billowing effect using the back of a spoon. Smooth and remove the excess buttercream from the sides with a palette knife, metal spatula or cake scraper to give a thick, smooth, striped look. Chill for at least 30 minutes before serving.

Top tip
The cashews will take on water in soaking and plumping, so half the basic recipe will be plenty. You may have a little extra, so make sure to measure out 450 g/1 lb. of the mixture.

Chocolate & pumpkin Halloween cake

400 g/14 oz. pumpkin or squash flesh, cut into cubes, steamed and cooled
315 g/scant 2½ cups plain/all-purpose flour
185 g/scant 1 cup caster/superfine sugar
3½ teaspoons baking powder
1¼ teaspoons bicarbonate of soda/baking soda
3½ tablespoons unsweetened cocoa powder
1 tablespoon pumpkin pie spice or mixed/apple pie spice
320 g/1½ cups soya/soy yogurt
120 ml/½ cup sunflower oil
1½ tablespoons golden/light corn syrup
1 teaspoon pure vanilla extract

DECORATION
40 g/1½oz. white vegan chocolate, chopped
225 g/8 oz. dark/bittersweet vegan chocolate, chopped
vegan orange food colouring (see page 11)
½ quantity of Simple Vegan Vanilla Buttercream (see page 20)
4 mini dried pumpkins (available online)
few mint sprigs
few thyme sprigs
vegan gold lustre spray
3 x 18-cm/7-inch cake pans, greased and lined
disposable piping/pastry bag
1 baking sheet, lined

Serves 20

Preheat the oven to 180°C (350°F) Gas 4.

Blitz the pumpkin in a food processor until mostly smooth. Set aside. Sift the flour into a bowl. Mix in the sugar, baking powder, bicarbonate of soda/baking soda, cocoa and mixed spice. Make a well in the middle.

Put the yogurt into a bowl, add the sunflower oil, syrup and vanilla, and mix with a spoon. Pour into the well in the dry ingredients. Fold through until smooth. Fold through the squash until combined.

Transfer to the greased and lined pans. Bake for 30–35 minutes until an inserted cocktail stick/toothpick comes out clean. Leave to cool in the pans for 10 minutes, then transfer to wire racks to cool completely.

For the spider web bark, melt the white chocolate and 100 g/3½ oz. of the dark chocolate in separate heatproof bowls set over a pan of simmering water (or microwave in 30-second bursts, stirring in-between). Working quickly, fill the disposable piping/pastry bag with the melted white chocolate. Spoon the melted dark chocolate onto the lined baking sheet and spread it out to a square with a palette knife or metal spatula. Snip the very tip from the piping/pastry bag of white chocolate and use it to pipe 4–5 spirals onto the dark chocolate. Drag a cocktail stick/toothpick through the spirals from the centre to the edge to create a web effect. Chill until set. Break into shards and chill until needed.

If necessary, trim the tops of the cakes to make level. Stir the orange vegan colouring through the buttercream to make a mid-orange shade. Sandwich the cakes together using 300 g/10 oz. of the buttercream. The bottom side of the top cake should be facing up. Place the cake on a cake plate or cake board. Crumb coat (see page 12) the cake using the remaining buttercream. This will be your final coating, giving it a semi-naked look, so scrape off enough buttercream to reveal some of the sponge.

Meanwhile, melt the remaining dark chocolate. Pour the chocolate around the top of the cake, next to the edge, allowing it to trickle down the sides, then work in a spiral motion moving inwards to cover the top of the cake. Sweep across the top with a long palette knife/metal spatula.

Working quickly, push the bark into the cake and nestle 3 of the mini dried pumpkins into the chocolate. Using a dinner knife, spread a little chocolate onto the base of the 4th pumpkin and place it on top of the others. Decorate with the mint and thyme sprigs. Allow to set, then spray the pumpkins with the vegan gold lustre spray.

Muscat & prune fruit cake

A rich, modestly filled fruitcake to be enjoyed any afternoon with a cuppa, or ramp
up the indulgence factor and serve for Christmas and feed with extra Muscat.

150 ml/²/₃ cup muscat, plus
  2 tablespoons (optional)
175 ml/³/₄ cup orange juice
125 g/scant 1 cup dried mixed
  fruit
150 g/generous 1 cup prunes,
  chopped
315 g/scant 2¹/₂ cups
  plain/all-purpose flour
100 g/¹/₂ cup dark soft brown
  sugar
185 g/scant 1 cup light soft
  brown sugar
3¹/₂ teaspoons baking powder
1¹/₄ teaspoons bicarbonate of
  soda/baking soda
2 teaspoons mixed/apple pie spice
320 g/1¹/₂ cups soya/soy yogurt
120 ml/¹/₂ cup sunflower oil
1¹/₂ tablespoons golden/light
  corn syrup
1 teaspoon pure vanilla extract
few sprigs of rosemary (optional)
2 tablespoons caster/superfine
  sugar (optional)
975 g/2 lb. 2 oz. Simple Vegan
  Vanilla Buttercream
  (see page 20) made with
  325 g/11¹/₂ oz. vegan butter
  and 650 g/4²/₃ cups icing/
  confectioners' sugar
few fresh cranberries (optional)
deep 18-cm/7-inch cake pan,
  greased and lined with a
  4-cm/1¹/₂-inch collar
3 disposable piping/pastry bags
  fitted with a medium-large open
  (1-cm/³/₈-inch) star nozzle/tip,
  a medium open (7-mm/¹/₄-inch)
  star nozzle/tip and a small round
  (3-mm/¹/₈-inch) round nozzle/tip

Serves 12–14

Put the muscat and orange juice into a pan and gently bring to the boil.
Add the mixed dried fruit and the prunes. Bring to the boil and simmer,
stirring frequently, for 4 minutes. Remove from the heat and allow to
cool. It should be a thick, glossy liquid clinging to the plumped fruit.

Sift the flour into a bowl, add the sugars, baking powder, bicarbonate
of soda/baking soda and mixed/apple pie spice, and mix with a spoon to
combine. Make a well in the middle. Put the yogurt into a bowl, add the
sunflower oil, syrup and vanilla, and mix with a spoon. Pour into the well
of dry ingredients. Fold through with a spatula or wooden spoon until
smooth. Fold through the fruit along with the surrounding jammy liquid.

Transfer to the pan. Wrap the pan in a double layer of baking parchment
and tie with kitchen string/twine. Cover loosely with a square of baking
parchment. Bake for 55 minutes–1 hour 5 minutes. Allow to cool in the
pan for 20 minutes, then invert onto a wire rack to cool completely. Poke
holes in the top of the cake with a cocktail stick/toothpick. Drizzle over
the 2 tablespoons of Muscat, if using. Leave to soak for 2–4 hours.

Dip the rosemary (if using) in cold water, scatter over the sugar and
leave on a piece of baking parchment to dry out for 1–2 hours.

Crumb coat (see page 12) the cake using 250 g/9 oz. of the buttercream.
Place in the fridge for 15 minutes. Use 300 g/10¹/₂ oz. of the remaining
buttercream to coat the cake in a second layer. Smooth and remove
the excess buttercream with a palette knife/metal spatula.

Fill each of the piping/pastry bags fitted with the open star nozzles/tips
with 150 g/5 oz. of buttercream. Fill the piping/pastry bag fitted with
the small round nozzle/tip with the remaining buttercream.

Using the largest nozzle/tip, pipe a curled shell shape. Cover the 'tail'
with the next shell shape below, curling in the opposite direction. Pipe
a dotted line either side of this, using the piping/pastry bag fitted with
the small round nozzle/tip (squeeze the piping bag to create the dot and
drag downwards slightly to release). Next pipe a smaller double shell
pattern. Pipe a straight shell shape, angled inwards slightly. Cover the
'tail' of the first with the top of the second straight shell shape (again
angle inwards slightly). Continue with this pattern all around the cake.

Top with the frosted rosemary and the fresh cranberries, if using.

Index

Suppliers

Note: In most instances I have used spices and superfood powders to add natural colour. If liked, Sugarflair Paste Colours or Magic Colours Pro Gel Colourings can be used.

Always check labels of individual products before using, to check for any possible ingredient changes.

AMAZON www.amazon.co.uk/.com
Blue spirulina powder:
Coconut & passion fruit cake p.35
Knickerbocker glorious cake p.43
Easter cuddles nest cake p.132

Freeze-dried pink pitaya powder:
Coconut & passion fruit cake p.35
Knickerbocker glorious cake p.43
Cherry bake 'wow' cake p.58
Pumpkin Persian love cake p.79
Oil-painted buttercream cake p.123
Super-stylish cakesicles p.127
Easter cuddles nest cake p.132

Macha green powder:
Knickerbocker glorious cake p.43
Pumpkin Persian love cake p.79

BAKING TIME CLUB
www.bakingtimeclub.com
Vegan sprinkles:
Knickerbocker glorious cake p.43
Queen of Sheba cake p.92
Super-stylish cakesicles p.127
Metallic marvel cupcakes p.128
Easter cuddles nest cake p.132

BARNABAS BLATT GOLD
www.barnabasgold.com
(also sold by Amazon.co.uk/.com)
Edible gold leaf:
Squishiest ever chocolate cake p.83
Indulgent chocolate chip brownies p.88

CAKE DECORATING COMPANY, THE
www.thecakedecoratingcompany.co.uk
Gel colours (Pro Gel, Magic Colours):
Neopolitan cakes in jars p.124
Father's Day stout cake p.135

Edible gold paint (Metallic Edible Paint, Magic Colours):
Fab fault-line cake p.48

DOISY & DAM
www.doisyanddam.com
Vegan chocolate drops:
Easter cuddles nest cake p.132

Vegan mini eggs, Good Eggs:
Easter cuddles nest cake p.132

DR OETKER www.oetker.co.uk
Unicorn sprinkles:
Easter cuddles nest cake p.132

FREEDOM MALLOWS
www.freedommallows.com
Vegan marshmallows:
S'mores dip cake p.109

GREEN & BLACKS
www.greenandblacks.co.uk
Cocoa powder:
Vegan Chocolate Sponge base p.16
Vegan chocolate fudge icing p.23
Knickerbocker glorious cake p.43
Squishiest ever chocolate cake p.83
Indulgent chocolate chip brownies p.88
Red velvet cake p.91
S'mores dip cake p.109
Neapolitan cakes in jars p.124

HOLLAND & BARRETT
www.hollandandbarrett.com
Dried mixed fruit:
Muscat and prune cake p.139

Cashew nuts:
Cashew vanilla frosting p.23
Marbled go-nuts cupcakes p.57
Father's Day stout cake p.135

LINDT CHOCOLATE www.lindt.co.uk
Lindt Excellence range of 70%, 85%, 90% and 99% cocoa dark/bittersweet chocolate bars are made without any animal products:
Epic Black Forest cake p.39
Knickerbocker glorious cake p.43
Protein power squares p.61
Forget-me-not Prosecco jelly cake p.76

LOTUS BISCOFF
www.lotusbiscoff.com
Lotus biscoff biscuits and spread:
Lotus Biscoff traybake p.106
S'mores dip cake p.109

MADDOCKS FARM ORGANICS
www.maddocksfarmorganics.co.uk
Edible flowers:
Courgette/zucchini & lime cake p.44
Elderflower & lemon cakes p.71
Forget-me-not Prosecco jelly cake p.76

OREO COOKIES www.oreo.com
Oreo cookies:
Oreo cookie cake p.87

PANZERS www.panzers.co.uk
Courgette flowers/zucchini blossoms:
Courgette/zucchini & lime cake p.44

PIP & NUT www.pipandnut.com
Almond butter:
Soft vegan caramel sauce p.24
Chocolate & salted caramel chickpea cake p.84
Salted caramel drip cake p.97

PLANET ORGANIC
www.planetorganic.com
Vegan white chocolate
(iChoc vegan white chocolate):
Super-stylish cakesicles p.127
Protein power squares p.61
Knickerbocker glorious cake p.43

SAINSBURYS www.sainsburys.co.uk
Freeze dried raspberry pieces:
Pistachio, lime & raspberry wowzer cake p.53

SUGARFLAIR www.sugarflair.com
(also sold by Amazon.co.uk/.com)
Sugarflair paste colours:
Va va voom Veganary cake! p.119
Metallic marvel cupcakes p.128
Lemon & white chocolate Mother's Day cake p.131

WAITROSE www.waitrose.com
Freeze dried strawberry pieces:
Knickerbocker glorious cake p.43

Silver lustre spray:
Metallic marvel cupcakes p.128

WIKIN & SONS/TIPTREE
www.tiptree.com
Fruit jams/jellies:
Epic Black Forest cake p.39
Peanut butter & vegan jelly/jam cake p.54
Cherry bake 'wow' cake p.58

Acknowledgments

Thank you to, my rock, Giuseppe, as more covid lockdowns hit, your faith in me, support and patience (!) never dwindled. And to the little sparkling stars of joy that are my beautiful daughters, Elena and Sofia, who inspire me every day.

A huge thank you to Clare Winfield for photographing and capturing each cake so elegantly. I will always be so grateful for your unwavering dedication to creating a wonderful piece of artwork as well as showcasing each individual recipe perfectly.

To Amy Dunbar for swooping in for our last few shoots, not only for assisting in the kitchen wonderfully, but for also doing a fabulous job styling the chapter opener page for the 'Chocs Away' chapter. Beautifully done.

Thank you to Max Robinson for your wonderful prop styling; graceful and thoughtful. I couldn't have asked for more.

To Art Director Leslie Harrington, not only for your fantastic creative vision, but as we all got used to working remotely, your 'wow's!' and reactions as each image pinged through to you kept me going in the kitchen!

Thank you to Kate Reeves-Brown for your edits and checks, so super and efficient.

Thank you to all the lovely in-house team at RPS, Toni Kay, the brilliant Senior Designer on this book and of course to both Editorial Director Julia Charles and Publisher Cindy Richards, who amazingly let me loose on another book! Thank you once again for allowing a seed of an idea to blossom so freely.

To Gordon Ramsey Kitchen Nightmares, my work colleague, when a spot of midnight baking had to be done due to topsy-turvy days of daytime home-schooling and night-time working!

Mum, always full of infectious energy, although covid regulations kept you from helping out in the kitchen as much as you (and me!) would have liked. Just to know I have your constant support keeps me striving. Dad, for being you, knowing I can chat to you about anything from cake to DIY, cricket (!?) to theatre, is, well, just brilliant. I'm a very lucky lady. I love you both very much.